THE
GREAT
PROMISE

*A compelling war journal fuels a grandson's
mission to finish an unfulfilled promise.*

FREDERICK L. COXEN

ISBN-10: 1463702930
EAN-13: 9781463702939
Library of Congress Control Number: 2011919869
CreateSpace, North Charleston, SC

IMPERIAL WAR MUSEUM

"I have now had the opportunity to read through the journal entries in some detail. I found your grandfather's wartime account to be full of interest, as his descriptions of serving with the Royal Field Artillery contain many excellent details which researchers will undoubtedly find of historical value. His accounts of involvement in the early battles of the war, when both sides were more mobile and trench warfare had not yet set in, are particularly interesting. I am sure that our visitors will find the document of definite value and should therefore be pleased to accept this copy as a donation to our archive, where a hard copy will be preserved under your grandfather's name and made available for study."

Imperial War Museum
Documents and Sound Section

The soldier kneeling on the cover of the book is my grandfather, Captain Frederick G. Coxen.

PROLOGUE

On a balmy North Carolina spring day of 2009, I sat at my kitchen table, swamped by the conglomeration of memorabilia amassed by my deceased paternal grandparents. The tattered box of paper relics had been transferred to me via my older sister, having been previously stored away and forgotten in various family closets for more than fifty years.

My objective was to find my grandfather's World War One journal. Among the contents of the box were an English marriage license, a couple of cookbooks, a boyhood bible, newspaper clippings, and several military documents. Eventually, I uncovered a small, brown ledger; printed on the front cover was "Army Book 152 Correspondence Book (Field Service)".

I gently lifted the journal from the box and held it in my hands. For a brief time I just stared at it, reveling in the moment. I'll never forget the emotional sequence that followed. At first I was overcome by an exhilaration comparable to one might expect when uncovering a treasure chest or embarking upon an adventurous journey. This elation became intermingled with awe for the piece of history I was holding. However, these sentiments were soon overshadowed by the riveting realization that I was holding my GRANDFATHER'S journal; a journal written astutely in his own fluent, cursive hand, almost one-hundred years ago. The pages were yellowed and the penciled script faded (figure 1). Even so, I was still able to follow a narrative that proved to be both insightful and compelling.

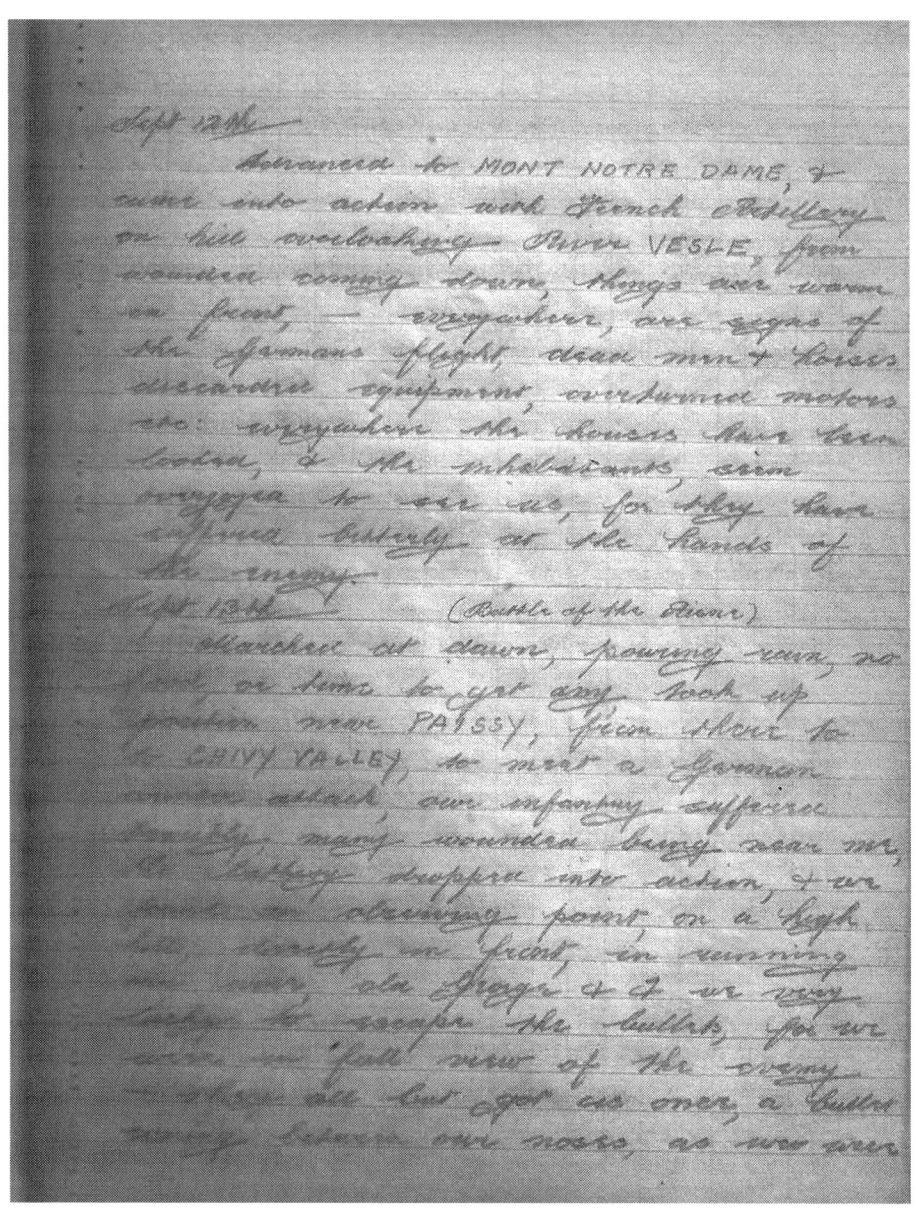

Figure 1

Thoroughly convinced of the value of this documentation, I aspired to transcribe the journal for other members of my family to enjoy, as well as to concretely preserve its contents for generations to follow. Countless hours were devoted to this undertaking — deciphering the colloquial and military language of a British soldier written a century earlier.

Progressing through the journal, I was able to transcribe my grandfather's experiences through late spring of 1915, following the second battle of Ypres. Knowing that the war continued through 1918, I was curious as to the reason why the entries suddenly ended. What changes in his military service might have taken place? How did he spend the remainder of the war? So, once again, I dove into the contents of our family carton searching for answers.

I was able to discover through other saved documents that, due to his specific skills and expertise, Frederick George Coxen had been assigned to other areas of responsibility for the duration of the war. None of this information had been revealed to me, or to my siblings, prior to this point.

By unraveling the poignantly historical threads of my grandfather's war years through the examination of his personal relics, I was able to sculpt together a more complete replica of the remarkably complex man he was.

I could not have anticipated that further excavation into the box contents would have had such a dramatic effect on the next few years of my life. Tucked away in the depths of all the memorabilia was a more recent correspondence of my grandfather's, typed on onion skin paper in 1945. The letter was addressed to no particular person or group; it just contained a title -

"I Had A Dream The Other Night"

It was one of those hazy, disjointed dreams that cause you on awakening to try to connect it in sequence, and leave you greatly perturbed in mind - yes, and in spirit.

It seems that I was sitting at a table - it might have been after a good dinner, for I felt quite satisfied with everything, and very complacent.

I leaned back in my chair, picked up a glass from the table, and was enjoying the odor of its contents - most likely an after-dinner brandy.

I seemed to hear a noise and looked up, and there stood three of my old buddies, "Pudgie" Taylor, Bobbie Glue, and George Bramwell. I seemed to become elated with a supreme sense of happiness, just as if I was suddenly transported into a kind of world hitherto unknown to me.

It appeared that we greeted each other with an enthusiasm beyond what we humans experience, and then it seemed that we all became rigid as Pudgie filled up glasses for each one of us.

We apparently stood a long time in silence, and then Pudgie spoke, just one of his utterances that I had heard so many times, "Here's to you, Old China" (in modern parlance: "Here's to you, old pal"). "May we all do the job together."

Then everything grew hazy, as it does in dreams, and I woke up. In the few moments it took to collect my senses, I was at first excited, then let down, "I have been dreaming." Memory took me over the years and thoughts drifted sadly.

Pudgie, Bobby, George, and I were old pals. A couple of days before the battle of Mons in August 1914, we promised each other that should one or more of us get back, we, or he, would call on the family of those who perished and explain how and when "it happened."

Within a few weeks of that pledge George was killed beside me at the Marne, and died in my arms. Pudgie got his at Ypres, repairing a telephone wire. Bobby's legs left his torso when I tried to pull him from our blown - in dugout, also at Ypres.

Since that enlightened dream the thought has been with me, "May we all do the job together." Pudgie meant, in forming that pact just prior to when the shooting started, that we all GET BACK TOGETHER.

Well, we didn't! Just one of the four did and that one failed to carry out the promise. For in the more than four years that the war continued, so much happened; time has gradually softened the memory, which is now one among so many.

Throughout the years I have had a great many dreams or mild nightmares fighting that war all over again, and have so often thought, "Was it worthwhile?" We positively know now, those of my generation who are left, together with the younger generation who are now engaged in completing the job more clearly how to see to it that it will be completed the RIGHT WAY this time.

I am wondering now, was that "visit" of my old buddies who have been lying in Flanders Fields for nearly thirty years, a reproach or a reminder? I don't know, but it has certainly caused my criticism of myself to assert itself. Were they not telling me that the job has to be done together?

Were they not asking, "Are we all united in our cause?" Were they telling me to do all I could to help COMPLETE the job which they and millions of others died for? It is all too complex for me to answer, but I do know one thing, and that very definitely, I HAVE NOT DONE MY BEST! I have made no sacrifice that could, in the smallest measure, be compared with that of the boys who are now going through that hell that I know so well.

Sure, I have done and am doing war work, getting well paid for it too. Sure, I have given time to selling war bonds, and bought some too. But I have to admit that I often get sore at the way the war is being run, like all the damn dumb things that make it cost so much, at the cockeyed forms that I have to fill in, and the taxes I have to pay.

I get mad too when I read and hear of strikes, when my gas is running low. I criticize about everything, EXCEPT TO PROMOTE THE ALL IMPORTANT FACT THE BOYS (as we fondly call them) ARE GOING THROUGH HELL AND DYING FOR FIFTY BUCKS A MONTH.

Dying for fifty bucks a month, that's what it amounts to, unless we of the home front do our part to back the fighting front, with every ounce of our individual strength, in dollars, work, and brains.

If we do not (even at the thought I would scream to high heaven), it will mean, as it did last time, veterans of war would be transformed into peddlers, aye, even beggars, yes, even worse, paupers, together with general chaos.

The question of "Why and for what did my old pals give their lives?" is still unanswered. May God grant that World War Two mold a different world than did World War One. We must see to it, or World War Three will develop. The irony of the thought of world war defined by numerals!

For a few days my dream sort of worried me. But I am grateful now, because it gave me reasons to do a little more thinking, the result of which gives me determination to try in every way to do a little more. Candidly, there is not much I can do in comparison to the sacrifice others are making, but I can and will work harder, count to ten before I start bellyaching, conserve, and save (that word "save" is right up my alley) for I can really do that by BUYING WAR BONDS TO THE UTMOST.

From now on I am going to ask myself a question very often, the question being "What did I do today for the one who may die for me tonight?" The answer, "I bought an extra bond."

Thanks for the visit, George, Bobby, and Pudgie; may you forever rest in peace, together with those who are joining you now.

By the Grace of God, and our efforts, perhaps we can make sure that my grandsons will not have to make the sacrifice you, and thousands who are now joining you, were called upon to make.

It took a while to digest the content of the letter and even longer to comprehend its full meaning. I started to imagine at what point in time these young men entered into their pact. The setting could have been on a train enroute to the Belgian frontier, or during the long march to their first engagement in Mons. Perhaps it was the trepidation from hearing the first barrage of heavy artillery prior to battle that drove the moment. Whenever or wherever it took place, these chums felt compelled to formulate a promise to each other and or a vow to notify one another's family in the event that he, or they, became a fatality of war. No one will know the emotional rationale behind the promise made that day; nevertheless, the letter does reveal that, as the lone survivor, my grandfather neglected to honor their covenant.

This letter testifies to the fact that Frederick G. Coxen, although very grateful for surviving the war, remained haunted by that fervent agreement made among friends - one devised by naïve, untested warriors, who could never have imagined the agonizing inferno they were about to face. My grandfather's dream epitomized the residual guilt he carried all those years, surmising that he had disappointed his chums.

Upon reviewing this revealing personal confession, I immediately became determined to fulfill my grandfather's promise, to locate and inform the descendants of those fallen soldiers.

Having now become acquainted with his war exploits, I can only imagine the terror and hardship my grandfather faced each day. By sharing his journal with you, along with the aspects of my search for these three families, you may come to understand the compelling reasons for committing myself to this quest, as well as to ascertain the likely motives behind leaving his promise unfulfilled.

DEDICATION

To my grandfather, Captain Frederick George Coxen, who served in the British Royal Field Artillery and the Royal Air Force during World War I. I also dedicate this story to the living relatives of George Bramwell, Pudgie Taylor, and Bobby Glue.

CONTENTS

PREFACE

This book is based on the World War One journal written by my grandfather, Captain Frederick G. Coxen, who was born in 1887 in London England and served in the Royal Field Artillery (RFA) and the Royal Air Force (RAF) from 1905 to 1919. At the age of 17 he began his military career in the RFA Special Reserves, and then on August 5, 1914, was called into active duty when the general mobilization decree was issued. He reported for duty at Newcastle and was assigned to the newly created Fortieth Battery of the 43rd Brigade. By August 16th the brigade had been sent over to France as part of the British Expeditionary Force (BEF).

The Great Promise is a memoir account of the following battles: the first battle of Mons, the first battle of Marne, the first battle of Aisne, the first and second battles of Ypres, and the battle of Neuve Chapelle. Each chapter in the book represents a battle and begins with a brief overview of the battle, intermingled with dramatic journal entries. This format helps establish a foundation for understanding the relationship between the journal entries and the battles they describe. Journal excerpts and other supportive documents are italicized and indented to assist with identification and clarity.

ACKNOWLEDGMENTS

I would like to acknowledge the debt I owe to those who diligently assisted me in my attempts to find information about George Bramwell, Pudgie Taylor, and Bobby Glue. I also wish to express a novice researcher's gratitude to the following websites for expanding my World War One knowledge: The Long, Long Trail; The Western Front Association; The British National Archives; Great War Forum; and FirstWorldWar. com. I am grateful to The Royal Imperial Museum in London for dedicating a copy of the journal to my grandfather. My eternal gratitude to my wife Lynne, whose contributions' made this book a reality. In addition, I'm appreciative to Dick Gordon and his staff for allowing me to present my story on the NPR radio program *The Story*.

INTRODUCTION

On a cloudless summer day in 1914, the men of the Fortieth Battery of the Royal Field Artillery heard what sounded like thunder as their wagon line approached its assigned artillery position. Each man deduced that it was not the rumbling of an oncoming storm but the sound of heavy artillery shells bursting over the town of Mons, Belgium. It was August 23, and the summer's heat turned both men and horses into mud figurines as the dust from the roads clung to their sweat-soaked bodies. When the wagon line reached its mark, the men released the six-inch Howitzers from their limbers and rolled them into position. With guns manned and ready, the gunners waited anxiously for the order to fire. It was perhaps only five or ten minutes before the order would be given, but for those waiting, each minute seemed an eternity.

This interlude likely afforded some men an opportunity to reflect on their loved ones back home, yet most focused on the possible outcome of the events about to unfold. Undoubtedly, their primary emotion was fear. Could they withstand or survive being shot? Would they have the courage to stand their ground with shells exploding all around them? How would they react hearing the agonizing sounds of their country-men crying out in pain? The men's thoughts quickly returned to the present when the order to fire arrived.

The solemn atmosphere stood in sharp contrast to the prior, spirited zeal of being involved in a "real scrap", demonstrating how the enthusiasm of anticipation wanes with the reality of participation.

CHAPTER ONE:

THE FIRST BATTLE OF MONS

In August of 1914, the British Expeditionary Force (BEF), under the command of Sir John French, boarded ships in the port city of Southampton, England for the short trip to Boulogne, France. The BEF were reluctant partners of the Allied Army commanded by the French Commander-in-Chief Joseph Joffre.

At Joffre's request, Sir John French agreed to move his army towards the Belgian town of Soignies. There he would cover the left flank of the French Fifth Army commanded by General Lanrezac. Sir John calculated that his army would arrive in Soignies on August 23.

The German First Army, commanded by General von Kluck and the Second Army commanded by General Bulow, had been fighting their way through Belgium. Von Kluck's First Army was marching towards Soignies, and would arrive on August 23.

On August 22, forward cavalry patrols of both the British and German armies encountered each other outside the city of Soignies. The German Hulans[1] turned to escape back to Soignies with the British in pursuit. They caught the Hulans in Soignies; following a brief skirmish all but one Hulan was killed.

When the British patrol reported their encounter, Sir John French surmised that he was facing the German First Army. He was reluctant to attack without knowing the enemy's strength, so he decided instead to take defensive positions along the Mons Canal. He ordered General

---

1   Hulans: A type of German cavalry that used long lances

Haig's First Corps to form a defensive line east of the city, while General Smith-Dorrien's Second Corps secured positions to the west.

Von Kluck was surprised to hear that he was facing the British BEF. He learned that the British were in France as stated in a Belgian newspaper, but he thought they were still somewhere near the coast. His battle plan was to attack the British west flank, but this would require that he move his army a short distance to the west away from the German Second Army. To proceed with this plan would require permission from General Bulow. Upon receiving the request, Bulow was fearful that a gap might develop between their two armies, offering the enemy an opportunity to flank them. He denied the request. Therefore, von Kluck was forced to launch a frontal attack the following day. On August 23, 1914, at 9:00 a.m., the German artillery opened fire on the British Second Corps. Although the First Corps was not directly involved in the fight, its artillery helped support the Second Corps success in repelling the first German attack.

The British forces with 70,000 men and 300 pieces of artillery were engaging an enemy with 160,000 men and 600 guns. When the battle commenced, the British found themselves heavily outnumbered in both men and artillery. Nevertheless, they were able to repel von Kluck's first attack by inflicting heavy casualties. Due to heavy losses, von Kluck decided to wait for his reserves to arrive before launching a second attack.

During this pause Sir John French received a message from the French General Lanrezac, it reporting that on August 22 the French Fifth Army attacked the German Second Army at Charleroi. General Lanrezac went on to state that his losses were significant and he feared envelopment.[2] Consequently, his Fifth Army was retreating.

Immediately Sir John French perceived that the withdrawal of the French Fifth Army meant exposure to his right flank, increasing the risk of the BEF being surrounded. He then ordered a strategic and orderly retirement from the battlefield, heading south.

---

2   Envelope: To be surrounded by the enemy.

Trip to the Belgium Frontier

Journal Entry - August 23rd

We dropped into action at Mons and as we moved into position, I could hear the sounds of heavy artillery guns. I could feel my excitement grow as I sensed the urgency in the voices and the movements of the battery crews rushing to get their guns into position. When all the guns were ready, I felt calmness settle over the area and I took this moment to take in all the sights and sounds around me as if painting a panoramic scene.

Suddenly I was jolted back into the present when our batteries started firing.

It was evening before the guns fell silent, allowing us to move forward towards a ridge that offered a decent view of the continuing battle in and around Mons. I stood on the ridge and stared at the battle below and thought to myself how thrilling it all seemed.

Then as the day faded into darkness, I was enchanted like a child viewing a fireworks display, watching the German shells burst above the battlefield. We fired a few more rounds before we packed up and returned to where we had bivouacked the previous night.

Arriving at the bivouac site, Fred rolled out his wool blanket and lay on the ground, using his saddle as a pillow. The heat of the day had been replaced by the cool night air, sending a chill through his tired body. He wrapped himself up in a second blanket and stared into the ebony, star-filled sky.

The horizon was occasionally illuminated by the light of an exploding shell, but otherwise, Fred lay in total darkness. He reflected on the day's events, interrupted by sentimental thoughts of home.

Eighteen days following mobilization passed so quickly he hadn't fully absorbed their impact on his life. Alone now without anything to interrupt his thoughts, it seemed a perfect opportunity to reflect upon the whirlwind of events spiraling him into his present situation. He fumbled in the darkness to retrieve his journal from the saddlebag, carefully removed it, and searched for a candle. With both items in hand, he draped a blanket over his head, while sitting cross-legged on the ground. Securing the blanket so as to block any outgoing light, he pulled a box of matches from his pocket and lit the candle. The flame provided a faint glow that enabled him to read some of his earlier journal entries.

He settled upon his August 4th posting, in which he elaborated upon his wife informing him of the mobilization decree. He had been so shocked by this news that he had insisted on viewing the document for himself. With his wife and baby in tow, Fred nervously hurried to the local post office to read the posted general mobilization order.

August 4th

"General Mobilization", will it be declared? This was the thought with me all day, after my dear wife first gave me the news. But then I could not believe it, until we walked to the post office and saw the official declaration. Then I knew I would have to leave my home and dear ones — for "Where", that was my one great thought. Until then I never realized what it all meant.

With the conflicting thoughts of my dear ones, along with fascination that I was going to participate in a "real scrap", my mind was in a real whirl, and was so until I left home the next day for Newcastle on the Tyne. And then — "Where?"

On August 5th I was to report for duty, so my wife and dear baby daughter walked with me to the train station where I was to catch the train to Newcastle.

Reviewing these past entries, Fred became overcome by sadness caused by leaving his dear ones at the train station. His eyes grew moist as melancholy enveloped him. How astonishing that it had happened so quickly — first the general mobilization and then the order to report for duty the next day. There hadn't been time to adjust to the separation from his family.

Determined to lift his veil of gloom, Fred continued reviewing his journal, detailing his train journey to Newcastle. The train car had been filled with other animated reservists, fueling an electrifying atmosphere. It seemed more celebratory than solemn, an unexpected frame of mind for men about to go to war.

Most were young lads in their teens or early twenties. They were naively stimulated by a passion for adventure, unaware of the grim realities of war. Even though Fred was leaving a young family, he too had become intoxicated by the elation, as evidenced by the following journal entry.

August 5th

I did not dwell on the thoughts of leaving my dear little wife, my mother, and baby — the journey up north was one of enthusiasm, for the train was packed with reservists, rejoining the Colours, as I. All seemed absolutely mad to go and obliterate Germany!

Fred continued reading his journal entries, recalling the events that took place upon arriving at Newcastle. How distressing it was when he had been initially assigned to the 39th Battery.

August 6–7th

Upon arriving I had to draw a kit from supply and then on to the doctor in order to pass my physical. Upon doing so, I was detailed to join the 39th Battery, assigned to Surplus Details, as acting Quarter Master Sergeant at Borden Camp. I was very disappointed, for this meant that I should not go to the front yet.

Later I was informed that I would be part of the nucleus of a Reserve Brigade that was being formed at Shorncliffe. I arrived at Borden and ran into my old commanding officer who seemed to feel great satisfaction in seeing me.

I immediately volunteered for active service but had a little trouble getting past the red tape, until seeking help from Brigadier Clark. It wasn't long after that I was assigned to the First Corps, 43rd Brigade, First Division at Deepcut. I was to

*report for duty on the 14th of August. After reporting in, I was
so glad to meet a couple of chums that were also assigned to
the 40th Battery RFA.*

Fred reflected upon the August 16th passage, citing when the First
Corps, which included the Fortieth Battery, had boarded a ship that
would take them to France.

*We embarked at Southampton on the SS City of Chester. It
was an uneventful trip over the channel to where we disem-
barked the next morning at Boulogne, France. I knew well that
I was in France, from the grand reception we received.*

After disembarking, the men fell into formation and marched to
their assigned rest camp outside Boulogne. Fred had noted that, after
a couple of days, the men were getting restless while waiting to be
shipped to the front.

August 17–19th

*In rest camp outside Boulogne we thought it very tame for
Active Service. We were anxious to test our skills and engage
the Germans.*

As indicated by his August 20 entry, the soldiers boarded a train that
would transport them to an unknown destination. Fred recalled how
he had gazed out the train's window as it passed through Amiens and
other towns along the way. Whenever the train stopped at a station, the
grateful inhabitants of the town would be waiting to display appreciation
for their arrival.

*Every station was crowded with people who showered flowers,
chocolate, smokes, and drinks of all kinds on the troops and
many Tommies[3] got their first kiss from a French lady.*

---

3   **Tommy:** Slang word for a British soldier.

Fred continued to peruse his journal entries. This brought to mind the night the men detrained at Macquigny, France, at which point they began their march to the Belgian frontier. They had received a splendid greeting at every village they passed through, enroute to the fortified village of Maubeuge, Belgium.

August 21st

Everywhere the French people gave the troops a hearty welcome, and then it occurred to me that just perhaps the people may have realized more than us what events were impending.

While halted outside Maubeuge, the French caught a woman with two pigeons concealed in her basket; one she had already dispatched without ceremony. The French shot her in a field just on our left.

By the time he finished reading the last journal entry, fatigue had crept over his tired body. The diminishing wick of his candle forced Fred to extinguish the flame or risk setting his blanket on fire.

Opting for the former, he replaced his belongings and prepared for a needed rest. Nestled within his blanket, he laid his head on his saddle and drifted off to sleep.

As night faded into morning Fred awakened to the disturbing sounds of the continuing battle, as well as the clamor of complaining horses whose handlers were hitching them to their limbers. Mounting his steed, Fred joined the wagon line that was on its way towards the previous day's gun positions.

Once the guns were positioned, the battery began firing at selected targets, but unlike the previous day, the enemy artillery was returning fire.

Aug 24th

One section of the battery was sent to shell a village near the town of Mons, but they all got captured or "put-out," except for a few.

A large force of Germans came within a couple hundred yards of where these few were hiding. Owing to a rise in the ground, they fortunately got safely away and rejoined the battery about noon.

When the enemy resumed their attack, Sir John French ordered the frontline of the Second Corps to fall back to their secondary defensive line. Knowing that they couldn't maintain their position much longer, he ordered the commencement of a full retirement from the battle field.

Although his order was not well-received by the soldiers, Sir John knew that had they remained they would fall to the enemy.

General Smith-Dorrien ordered his Second Corps to break-off all engagements with the enemy and begin an orderly retirement south towards the town of Le Cateau, Meanwhile General Haig's First Crops marched southeast to Landrecies.

Aug 24th

It was due to the splendid aerial reconnaissance of our aviators that saved our army. For without them we would have been outflanked and the result too awful to imagine. However, the troops on the whole were greatly against the idea of running away, but we had to thank our splendid leaders for the way the gigantic thing was carried out. It was indeed marvelous.

We incurred very heavy losses, but the Germans did not have it all their own way, for they paid dearly for every mile of ground they gained.

The battle of Mons

Soignies

Mons

Maubeuge

Aulnoye

Sambre R.

brai

Marbaix

Avesnes

Le Cateau

CHAPTER TWO:

THE RETIREMENT SOUTH

The soldiers of the Second Corps were exhausted from fighting and marching without food or water in the intense summer heat. To make matters worse, von Kluck kept harassing them with a constant artillery bombardment which forced the British to perform several rearguard actions.

General Smith-Dorrien entered Le Cateau ahead of his army to meet with his forward scouts. They reported that the enemy had already occupied the high-ground around the city.

The newly-arrived Fourth Corps came along side of the Second. General Smith-Dorrien considered the overall exhaustion of his troops, fearing that the enemy would soon overtake them if they continued retreating. He believed that survival required them to take an immediate defensive stand. However, doing so would constitute disobeying a direct order from Sir John French. He gathered his commanders and reached a consensus regarding his proposal. He then approached General Snow, commander of the Fourth Corps. Upon achieving his support, preparations for battle began.

Help was elicited from the men and women of La Cateau to dig shallow trenches for the troops. On the morning of August 26 the German artillery opened and maintained fire for several hours. When the bombardment ceased, the British watched as wave after wave of German infantry marched towards their lines.

From their shallow trenches the British responded with rapid and accurate fire, inflicting heavy damage on the advancing enemy. By late afternoon the enemy eventually breached sections of the British line. However, the valiant effort of his men gave General Smith-Dorrien time to design an organized retirement. As evening approached, he decided the time was right to disengage the enemy and restart their retirement south. Because of heavy casualties the Germans did not pursue the retreating British forces. Nevertheless, von Kluck continued the chase the next morning.

While the Second Corps fought in Le Cateau, the First Corps was approaching their billet in Landrecies. They had marched for hours in the heat with a minimal amount of water. Fred was so tired that he often fell asleep in his saddle. Fortunately, his well-trained charger dependably trudged along behind the preceding line of horses. Occasionally, Fred would gaze around from atop his horse to contemplate the long line of slowly advancing men. It was difficult for him to imagine that only a few days earlier their uniforms had been clean and each man had exuded an air of confidence. Now, after days of fighting and long hours of marching in relentless heat, every man's uniform was dirty and in disarray. The flame of self-assurance that had once burned brightly in the men's eyes had been extinguished, transformed into a glazed display of weary desperation.

Retirement from Mons

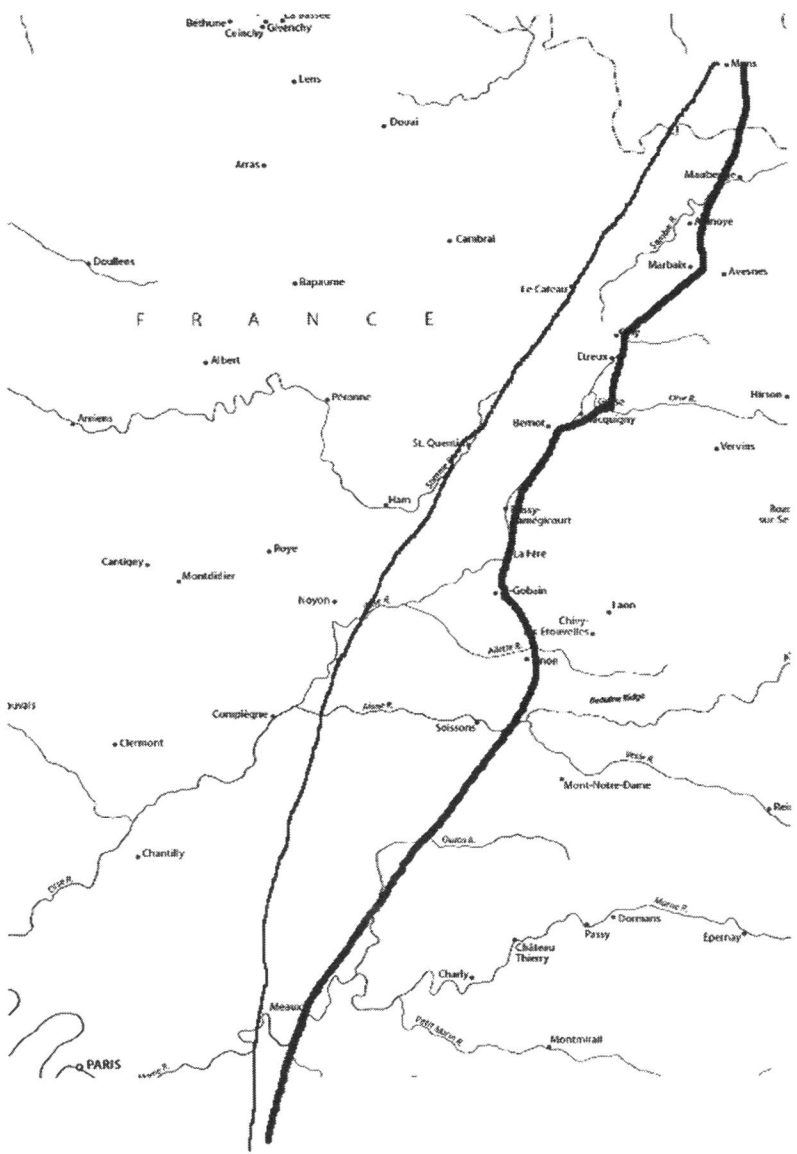

The bold line is the retirement track of the BEF First Corps while the other shows the path of the Second Corps.

August 25th

British rear guard action at Fugnies; the battery stampeded the enemies' supply column.

After an unnerving day of alarms—finally bivouacked.

August 26th

We marched 20 miles from early morn to late at night through the towns of Marbaix, Gohelle, and into Oisy, France. Although it rained all night, by midday, we ran out of water for the horses as well as the infantry.

I felt sorry for the poor chaps in the infantry, for they had to march for so long in the heat and dust from the road without water. When possible our battery would give them a lift on our wagons, horses, or vehicles. We were marching from dawn to dark trying to increase the distance between us and the Germans. By the time we stopped that night I was delighted to get out of my saddle and stretch my legs.

On August 27 the First Corps continued south. Periodically the artillery battery went into action against the pursuing Germans, trying to hamper their progress.

August 27th

We marched 23 miles via Etreux, Guise, to Bernot and on the way we came into action several times to cover our retirement from the German attacks.

At each town, along the path of the retiring British army, citizens were in the process of evacuating before the Germans arrived. The enemy was known for its brutality against innocent civilians. When the BEF entered the town of Guise, the streets were crowded with fleeing inhabitants attempting to salvage as many belongings as possible.

Hearing the sound of artillery exploding on the outskirts of town, the disorganized exodus became a mass panic. The British had to force the villagers off the road so that the troops could remain ahead of the advancing Germans.

August 27 continued

It was pitiful to see the horror-stricken faces of the refugees at Guise. They were trying to remove what they could carry or transport by cart in their rush from town. As the Germans came into one end of town, we left from the other end.

After days of almost continuous marching the men were exhausted from the lack of food and water. With the enemy aggressively pursuing them, supplies were difficult to obtain. The men ate what rations remained or they foraged for food wherever available.

We marched all night and I was getting extremely hungry, but food was very scarce. When the column stopped to water the horses, I decided to ride about to forage for food; I was lucky to find a bakery nearby. I rode my charger over to the shop and managed to secure a loaf of bread. I ate half of it, without butter, and put the remainder in the horse's nose bag so that I could eat it the next day. Once the horses were watered, the column continued to march south. Around midnight we found a field to bivouac in.

When the column stopped for the night Fred turned over his charger to one of the horse handlers, then headed off in search of his chums. This presented quite a challenge; how would he find anyone in this mass of humanity in the pitch darkness? He couldn't even see his hand in front of his face! After stumbling over a few sleeping bodies and receiving life-threatening exclamations as a result, he disappointingly gave up the hunt.

Luckily he remembered depositing his saddle near one of the limbers. After orienting himself along the wagon line, he managed to clumsily execute a successful search, for to his startled relief, he eventually tripped over his saddle. Once he secured the necessities for a brief respite, he mentally withdrew from the day's events and fell asleep. At first light everyone began to move about in preparation for another day of marching. Fred drowsily looked around and was amazed to spot his chums no more than ten feet away. As he recounted his feeble attempt to locate them the night before, they all enjoyed a hearty laugh.

August 28th

We started marching at 4:30 a.m. and came into action near Brissy to help cover our retirement. Later we helped support Scots Greys and infantry fighting their way across the river. The weather is very hot and everybody, men and horses, was dead tired.

August 29th

After marching 34 miles from Guise, our retirement slowed and we had a rather easy day of it. I took a needed short rest and a wash. During this time we overhauled the telephones and other equipment. When we reached Saint-Gobain we heard news that 600 Manchester Fusiliers and a section of the 118th Battery were wiped out.

The First Corps was still being pursued by the Germans. The men were able to stay ahead of the enemy's main body by out-marching them. They continued their retirement southward towards Paris in hopes of rallying with the French army, in order to make a defensive stand.

August 30th

The march of 33 miles from Saint-Gobain to Pinon was very long and hot, but we were lucky to bivouac on the grounds of a lovely chateau, where I took a refreshing dip in the lake.

On the morning of August 31st they left their position at Pinon and marched for five days. Covering sixty-five miles they reached Coulommiers, France by September 4.

August 31st

My day started at 3:30 a.m. when we were called to formation for our day's march. The coolness of the early morning air helped the column keep a steady pace. By midday the pace slowed as the oppressive heat took its toll on both the men and horses. Every time we came to a halt, many of the infantry would fall to the ground from fatigue, viewed in various sleep positions - sitting up, standing up, or lying down.

I was more fortunate for I could sleep a few hours on and off while sitting in the saddle. We continued to march all day until stopping late that night.

September 1st

Marched at 5:30 a.m. At dawn, near the city of Compiegnie, France, the Germans attacked our rear and L Battery was knocked out. We were lucky because we moved just in time, and we did not know how near we were to being put out until later.

Long march to Marolle Bridge. At 6:30 p.m. I went to sleep by my saddle. We were aroused by alarm at 11:30 p.m. to move, for engineers were waiting to blow up the bridge. We got across just in time and up went the bridge. German Cavalry were very close, so we marched through the night and halted on the roadside about 3:00 a.m. It was less than a minute and I was sound asleep on a friendly heap of stones.

Up again, marching again. How I longed for a sleep — anywhere. Continued retirement; reached the city of Meaux at 5:30 a.m.

September 2nd

Marched via Varreddes, Germingny, and bivouacked near Jouarre - it was a long, hot, and weary march.

September 3rd

Halted nearly all day east of Sammeron. The rear guard was slightly engaged, and the weather remains very hot.

September 4th Marched to Coulommiers, bivouacked early, and washed my underclothing. Thought we were going to have a day's rest, but had to move quickly in the morning in order to take up position SW of Coulommiers. We dug in and remained in action all night, leaving position at dawn to march with Division to Rozny.

September 5th

In position at Rozny, no contact with enemy.

We hear that the retreat is over and with the French we are to advance. How glad we were — anything but that continual marching.

CHAPTER THREE

THE FIRST BATTLE OF MARNE

The British and French armies were exhausted. They had marched for ten to twelve days under constant German attack. At long last, the French commander in chief, Joseph Joffre, issued an order that the armies stop their retreat south of the River Marne. Sir John French was hesitant to follow Joffre's order until the British War Minister, Lord Kitchner, convinced him otherwise.

The German First and Second Armies were approaching Paris from the east. Commander Joffre ordered the French Sixth Army to attack the right flank of the German First Army. When the enemy turned to face the attack, it opened up a thirty-mile-wide gap between the two German Forces. Taking advantage of this opportunity, the French Fifth Army and the BEF slipped through the gap and attacked the right flank of the German Second Army.

The following paraphrased passages are from Sir John French's dispatches to his commander in chief regarding the Battle of Marne.

Sir John French's First Dispatch

On Saturday, September 5th, I met the French Commander in Chief at his request. He informed me of his intention to take the offensive forthwith, as he considered conditions were very favorable to success.

He announced to me his intention of using the French 6th Army by directing it to move on the Ourcq, cross the river, and attack the flank of the 1st German Army, which was then moving in a southeasterly direction east of that river.

He requested me to effect a change in the BEF's position in order to fill the gap between the French 5th and 6th Armies. I was then to advance against the enemy in my front and join in the general offensive movement. These combined movements were to commence on Sunday, September 6th, at sunrise; and on that day it may be said that a great battle opened on a front extending from Ermenonville, through Lizy on the Marne, Mauperthuis, which was about the British centre, Courtecon, Esternay, and Charleville, to a point north of the fortress of Verdun.

About the 3rd September the enemy appears to have changed his plans and stopped his advance upon Paris; for on the 4th September air reconnaissance showed that the German main columns were moving in a southeasterly direction. On the 5th September several of these columns were observed to have crossed the Marne.

The German troops, which were observed on the 4th moving southeast, were now reported to be halted and facing the

Ourcq River. Heads of the enemy's columns were seen crossing at Changis, La Ferte, Nogent, Chateau Thierry, and Mezy.

Considerable German columns of all arms were seen to be converging on Montmirail, whilst before sunset large bivouacs of the enemy were located in the neighborhood of Coulommiers, south of Rebais, La Ferte-Gaucher, and Dagny.

Sir John French's Second Dispatch

On the 7th September both the 5th and 6th French Armies were heavily engaged on the British Army's flank.

The 2nd and 4th Reserve German Corps on the Ourcq River vigorously opposed the advance of the French Army, but did not prevent the French 6th Army from gaining some headway, the Germans themselves suffering serious losses. The French 5th Army inflicted severe losses on the German Army, especially around Montceaux, thus forcing them back to the line of the Petit Morin River. The fighting was so fierce that the armies were engaged in hand-to-hand combat with bayonets. As we advanced, the enemy retreated and their Guard Cavalry Divisions suffered severely. Our Cavalry acted with great vigor, especially General De Lisle's Brigade with the 9th Lancers and 18th Hussars.

On the 8th September the enemy continued his retreat northward, and our Army was successfully engaged with the enemy on the Petit Morin River, thereby materially assisting the progress of the French Armies.

The First Army Corps encountered stubborn resistance at La Tretoire, just north of Rebais.

The enemy occupied a strong position with infantry and guns on the northern bank of the Petit Morin River. They were finally dislodged after suffering considerable losses. Several machine guns and many prisoners were captured, and upwards of two hundred German soldiers were left dead on the ground.

The forging of the Petit Morin at this point was much assisted by the Cavalry and the 1st Division, which crossed higher up the stream.

Later in the day the enemy counter attacked, but it was well repulsed by the First Army Corps; a great many prisoners and some guns again fell into our hands. On this day (8th September) the Second Army Corps encountered considerable opposition, but drove back the enemy at all points with great loss, making considerable captures. The Third Army Corps also drove back considerable bodies of the enemy's infantry and made some captures.

On the 9th September the First and Second Army Corps forced the passage of the Marne and advanced some miles to the north of it. The Third Corps encountered considerable opposition, and the enemy destroyed the bridge at La Ferte.

The enemy in strength occupied the opposite bank and was able to hold the town by obstructing the construction of a bridge. It was after nightfall before we were able to cross.

During the day's pursuit the enemy suffered heavy loss in the number of soldiers killed or wounded, while hundreds of prisoners fell into our hands. The 2nd Division captured a battery of eight machine guns.

The enemy increased his forces against the French 6th Army west of the Ourcq River, and very heavy fighting ensued. However, in the end the French were successful throughout. The 5th French Army reached the neighborhood of Chateau Thierry after the most severe fighting, having driven the enemy completely north of the river with great loss. The severe fighting continued in the neighborhood of Montmirail.

Our advance resumed at daybreak on the 10th, and we were opposed by the enemy's strong rearguard. We were able to drive the enemy northwards, and in the process thirteen guns, seven machine guns, about 2,000 prisoners, and quantities of transport fell into our hands.

The enemy left many dead on the field. On this day the French 5th and 6th Armies had little opposition.

As the 1st and 2nd German Armies were now in full retreat, this evening marks the end of the battle which practically commenced on the morning of the 6th instant, and it is at this point in the operations that I am concluding the present dispatch.

Although I deeply regret to have had to report heavy losses in killed and wounded throughout these operations, I do not think they have been excessive in view of the magnitude of the great fight, the outlines of which I have only been able very briefly to describe, and the demoralization and loss in killed and wounded which are known to have been caused to the enemy by the vigor and severity of the pursuit.

The battle of Marne

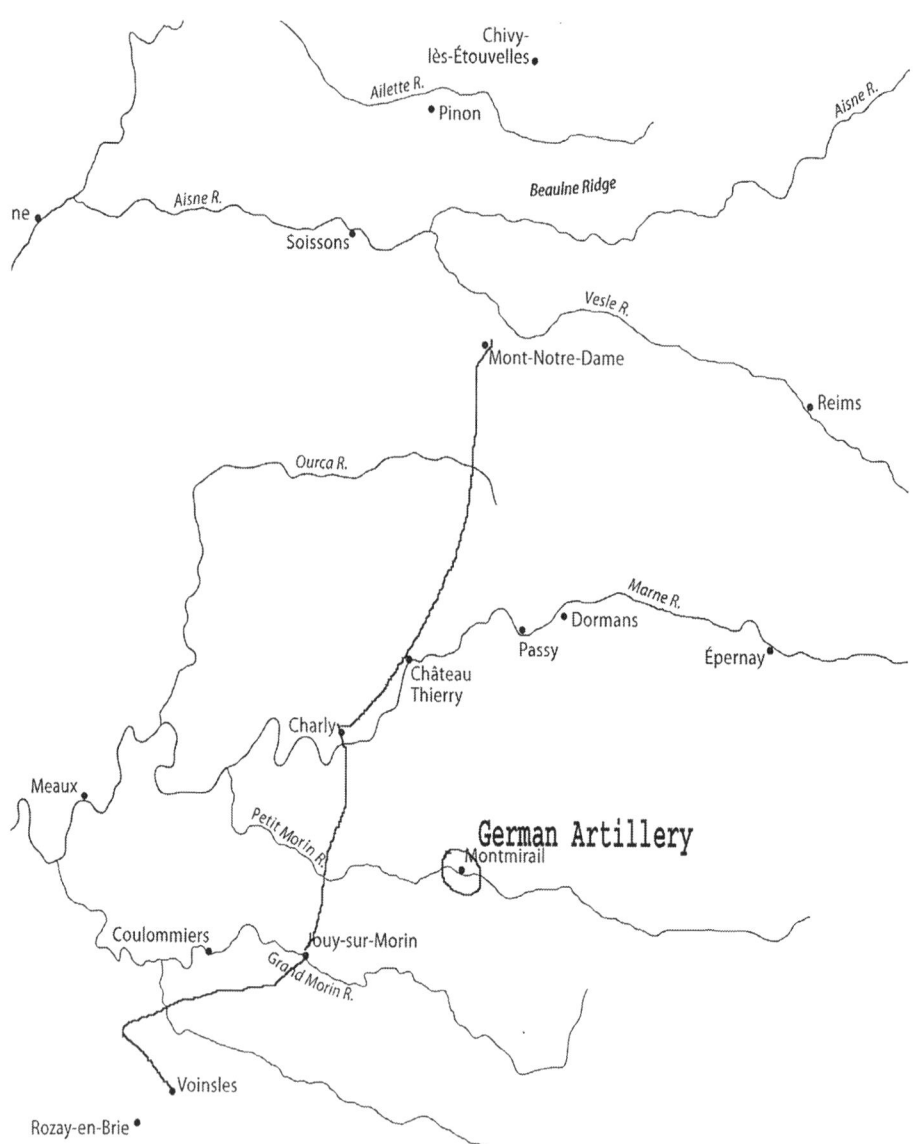

Journal Entry - September 6th

We occupied positions east of the town of Voinsles so that we could cover the advance of the 3rd and 5th Cavalry. As the Cavalry advanced, we moved our guns forward and occupied the line between Le Plessis and Andnoy.

On the way into Le Plessis I spotted a farmhouse and rode my charger over to the house to check it for provisions. I dismounted behind the house and went inside. I discovered that the Germans had destroyed the entire contents of the house, so I turned and left. The instant I stepped out the door a shell exploded close by.

I saw one of the Coldstream Guards die after being hit by a piece of shrapnel — the poor chap. I wondered if this means the breaking of a woman's heart, or had he little children? This set me thinking. My thoughts were all with my dear ones at home.

I shall always remember that hour, my real first initiation into the horrors of war. I cannot say I was afraid, yet it all seemed so strange.

But we were advancing the war. Our cry was, "We've got them on the run, and we are going to have our own back." Later in the day we advanced to a position south of Voudnoy and bivouacked.

September 7th

It was 3:45 a.m. when we started the march and joined the Advanced Guard to Faleys. On arriving we found that engagement was already in progress between our Cavalry and the enemy. The Cavalry forced the enemy to retreat before we could drop into action, so we continued our advance to Jouy-Sur-Morin.

September 8th

On our arrival at Jouy-Sur-Morin we were already engaged with the enemy on our front. We turned to find a German artillery battery firing at us from Montmirail. As the fighting continued, a thunderstorm formed. During the heavy rain and lightning the Germans retreated. That night we bivouacked in the rear of the 2nd Brigade and all night long we could hear the sounds of heavy fighting from the front.

September 9th

At 4:00 a.m. we marched with the Advanced Guard of the 3rd Infantry Brigade towards the Marne River. The Cavalry crossed first, and we finally stopped two and half miles north of Charly.

September 10th

At 6:00 a.m. we marched ahead of the main body and we were soon engaged in the thick of the fight that afterwards would be called the battle of the Marne. We dropped into action in the open. My chum and I ran our headphone wire over a small ridge from our observation post and then back to the battery. As we were running the wire a French Cavalry man galloped past me with blood running from himself and his horse.

I was about to connect my instrument when I heard a loud whining sound followed by a horrific explosion. It was our christening of heavy artillery fire, amounting to two hours of continual hell.

The Battle of Marne marked the first time the men of the Fortieth Battery had experienced direct bombardment in battle, where lives were lost. The men were forced to face the full impact of this level of engagement.

By World War One the development of heavy artillery far exceeded that of any previous war. Often, prior to an attack, intense artillery bombardment was used to soften the enemy's fortifications. Occasionally the effect of hours of intense shelling would cause the enemy to flee their positions. Fred experienced this lesson firsthand during a bombardment in the Battle of Marne.

September 10th - continued

Our forces came under heavy artillery fire for more than 2 hours and many of our infantry started to run. CRA General Finley and Colonel Sharpe tried to stop the retreat by urging the solders to turn and move forwards. In the process the General was killed and two officers were wounded.

The German artillery found the range of our battery and we came under heavy shelling. As shells were bursting all around me, I crouched beneath a gun limber. The whine of incoming shells followed by deafening explosions kept up for what seemed like an eternity.

Fear started to overcome my sense of duty and I had to force myself not to run. I don't know where or how I found the courage to stand up and yell out orders to the battery leaders so they could fire their guns.

As the Northampton and Sussex Regiments retreated through our battery they also drew the enemy's fire. During the infantry's mad rush they broke my telephone wire. I thought that my chum at the other end had gotten knocked over — he thought the same of me.

Without the ability to communicate with my chum on the other end, the battery guns couldn't fire.

To overcome this problem, we resorted back to using sema-phore flags[4] to pass down firing orders.

With things seemingly under control, I set out to mend the wire and restore communications. While I crawled along the ground following the wire, I could hear bullets pass over my head and striking the ground around me. Thank God the Germans were lousy shots! I found and mended the break just in time for the battery to help support the 60th Rifles' advancement. They were able to retake the position that the Northampton and Sussex regiments held prior to their retire-ment. As the 60th Rifles advanced, the enemy retreated. The regiment suffered heavy losses during this engagement.

September 12th

Our battery advanced to Mont Notre Dame, where we found a French Artillery unit already in action on a hill overlooking the Vesle River.

From our position we could see the enormous number of our wounded coming down the road from the front lines, which indicated to me that things were worse in front. Everywhere I looked I saw signs of the Germans' flight; dead men and horses, discarded equipment, and overturned motor cars.

We were driving the Germans back. As we passed houses the inhabitants who had suffered bitterly at the hands of the enemy seemed overjoyed to see us.

---

4   Semaphore Flag: Hand-held flags used as a method for sending.

CHAPTER FOUR:

THE FIRST BATTLE OF AISNE

The Battle of Marne marked a turning point in the war. The Allies stopped the German army from advancing farther into France. It is also significant to note that the Battle of Marne marked the onset of trench warfare.

After their defeat in the battle of Marne, the German army withdrew north toward the Belgian border. The Allied armies were slow in pursuing the retreating Germans, thus allowing them to build defensive positions at the Aisne River. The Germans selected a stretch of the river between the towns of Compiegne and Berry-au-Bac.

There the Germans occupied the high ground, digging trenches to enhance their defensive positions. In this area the Aisne River winds westward and is approximately one hundred feet wide, with depths that range from twelve to fifteen feet. The combination of width and depth made it impossible for the Allied army to cross on foot.

The topography of this stretch of river consists of low-lying ground that quickly rises into three to four-hundred-foot cliffs, creating ideal conditions for one of the most formidable positions on the western front. The Germans decided to occupy the higher northern side of the river about two miles from the crest of the cliffs.

Dense, thick brush covered the steep slope leading to the Germans' position. This made it difficult for an army to maneuver. The surrounding farm fields were flat and contained low-growing crops, which offered the Allies little cover when they made their attack on September 13.

On September 13th the BEF launched a frontal attack on the German positions across the river. The Allied forces had established a bridgehead by September 14th, allowing them to continue their assault. The German army tried to maneuver past the Allied forces by flanking them, forcing the Allies back across the river. In response, the Allied forces tried to outflank the German army. This perpetual leapfrogging tactic kept the two armies moving westward. It was called "The Race to the Sea", because it continued towards the French and Belgian port cities.

First battle of Ainse

Journal Entry - September 13th

Dawn came without food or the time to locate provisions, as we prepared to attack the enemy during a pouring rain. Our battery took up positions near Passy and from there we moved to Chivy Valley, where we waited for a German counterattack.

Our infantry suffered greatly, with many wounded, before our battery dropped into action. George Bramwell and I found an observing point on a high hill that was directly in front of the action. While running the wire back to the battery, George and I were very lucky to escape the bullets that were landing all around us. We were in full view of the enemy; once a bullet came between our noses as we did our best to duck while running the wire.

At one point the German artillery was shelling heavily all around us. George and I had to lay down to avoid being hit by shrapnel. The shelling continued into the afternoon and the sun was hot as we laid there unable to move. I must have been very tired for I actually went to sleep for a while. Later I was awakened when one of our staff officers was talking nearby. He must have thought I got bowled over because he was shocked when I started to move!

Upon finally reaching the battery, George and I hooked up the telephone then returned to the observation post. Together we found a rock that would work well for our observation post, once we removed the dirt from under it.

Later that day our selection of the rock proved to be a good choice, for it saved us from getting completely wiped out of existence during a heavy bombardment. Our battery fired heavily all day and into the night.

That night I remained on the hill for I was on guard duty. We had double sentries posted with orders to shoot anybody that approached without giving a prompt reply to the challenge.

Towards dawn I discovered that two of the sentries were missing. I had a very uncomfortable time searching for them, for the enemy was again very active. I was fortunate to find them before the enemy did.

September 14th

There was heavy fighting all day. Our little rock proved a haven of refuge when the Germans bombarded us with "coal-boxes".[5]

Some chaps dodged under our rock for shelter and gave us some of their tobacco, which worked out because until then I was both smokeless and foodless. My only feast today had been half a biscuit that was a left over from an emergency ration. During the shelling Major Johnson was killed and Major Murdock was slightly wounded.

September 15th

Today started out the same as yesterday, except the 113th and 46th Batteries on our left were abundantly shelled causing many casualties.

Hard fighting continued all day, so I was getting used to the thunder-like clap of the "coal-boxes" and other sundry missiles the Germans were flinging at us wholesale.

The German artillery is superior to ours in both the number of guns and in the size of the shells so we suffer greatly. At times when we are being heavily bombarded it sounds like hell let loose.

---

5   **Coal-box:** A type of artillery shell used by the German Army that produced a great deal of black smoke when it exploded. The black smoke looked like the dust produced when a box of coal is dropped.

September 16th

There has been heavy scrapping all morning long and into the afternoon.

To prevent the enemy from detecting our position, the battery took up another position a few miles away on the top of Mount Gourdon. This commanded a good view of the enemy's lines.

The battery was lucky they moved because an enemy observation plane spotted the battery at the old position. Upon reporting it, it was peppered with shells.

We exchanged shells with the Germans throughout the day, and when things quieted down I ventured out from our little rock. I was sickened to see all of the dead horses lying around.

As the day progressed, storm clouds moved in and by nighttime it started raining hard. We moved positions, and in the process I was wet through. By now I had gotten so used to it that when I was ready to sleep I just crawled under a gun limber. While lying there I thought to myself, "I would give anything for something hot to drink and some good food."

September 17th–October 13th

On the 20th of September I managed to get a little drop of water to wash my face, for it had not seen water for 8 days and I had not shaved for over a fortnight. I looked at myself in someone's little pocket mirror and thought, "What a picture I am."

We have effectively formed our battle line known as the Aisne River.

We've been fighting for a long period of time, all day and almost every night. It seems to come to one as second nature by now. We fired an average of 250 rounds each day. It is really similar to siege warfare, except instead of trying to scale a high castle wall, we try to scale the land between trenches.

Enemy attacks take place nightly. For protection from the shelling I dug a hole at the back of a limber as my home.

Every day seems to be alike. The only difference is that some days the fighting is more severe than others. They shell us occasionally so it is never safe to move far from our dugouts or the shelter of the guns.

The battery took up a position at the base of the cliffs where the Aisne River has eroded away some of the limestone creating great caves.

We placed our wagon train inside the caves for added protection, but even there we have had quite a few men wounded and several horses killed.

Sometimes when they shell us severely we have to desert the guns and take refuge in an adjacent cave. This undoubtedly has been the means of saving some lives.

One night I slept in the cave. Before dawn the next morning I was going to the guns like I do most mornings. However, this morning I left when it was still dark, lost my way, and wandered towards the enemy lines. When it became light I found that I had wandered into a valley between us and the Germans. I was confused and hardly knew what to do. I could hear rifle bullets whipping uncomfortably near me. The ground all around me was full of great holes that were caused by the German heavy artillery.

I knew that when it became full light I would be in a veritable death trap. I was hopelessly lost and unarmed so I decided to take refuge in a shell hole and wait throughout the day. Then when night fell I would try to make my way back.

As timed passed I decided I would chance it and either get to our own lines or meet whatever came my way. After a great deal of wandering and exciting moments, I met an officer who was forward observing. He directed me to where he thought our guns were located.

I reached our guns without further mishap. My off-man and the others thought I had gotten swallowed up for nobody saw me go. Strangely the path I had taken from the cave took me within 10 yards of our guns, which I could see well in the daylight. We all had a good laugh.

October 9th

This day was going to be well-remembered. During the morning things were a little more quiet than usual. We were sitting around the guns. I had left my telephone beneath one of the gun limbers.

We were having a feast of Bully Beef[6] and potatoes (potatoes did not come our way often), when a battery of German artillery found us with shrapnel shells.

The first round burst directly over our number three gun, which was just a short distance from us. Needless to say we all scattered. Bramwell and I ran towards the gun limber where I left the field phone. George was to my right when I heard the shell burst and saw him go down.

I dove under the limber to phone my chum Collins, while two gunners dragged Bramwell to the shelter of the limber. It was just seconds after they delivered him when three more shells exploded and the two gunners went down.

---

6   **Bully Beef:** Canned corned beef that was the principal protein ration of the British army.

Collins came running, and he and I did what we could for poor Bramwell but it was useless. Bullets from bursting shells hailed down on the limber as I held him in my arms. Collins and I expected to be hit any second but the limber saved us.

After the shelling stopped we removed poor Bramwell; it was an unpleasant sight to see a chum's brains by one's side. Once Bramwell's body was removed, I noticed that a shell case was stuck in the ground just two yards from where I laid. Luckily it didn't splinter, for Collins and I would have been killed. Everything seemed to bear marks of that lively hour excepting for us two.

We dug a hole that night and many times the hole saved us. When it was comfortably quiet, invariably the enemy would switch over and shell us. Several men were wounded at different times when it was least expected.

About this time, night attacks were very frequent and severe. Often there would be three attacks during the night.

Several times my wire was broken by shellfire somewhere between the guns and our observation point. To solve this problem Collins and I ran a double line, but in spite of it, we were forced to venture out to repair one of them when it was unhealthy to do so.

On the morning of the 8th of October a coal-box dropped near number five gun, killing one gunner and wounding four others.

We were shelled in the afternoon and they flung no fewer than 40 "dud" shells over us in an hour.

I found it was rather amusing to feel the thud when the shell struck the earth with no explosion ensuing. During the shelling we lost several horses on the wagon line while several others were wounded.

Since we were being shelled so often, the Major sent out a party to prepare a new position but they were shelled out.

That night the Major asked us if we would prefer to move because the position was warm. We decided to stay. Our place was as good as another.

After the battle of Aisne, the British forces were exhausted. They entered into a period of rest, while the French continued to engage the Germans in the" Race to the Sea". However, Winston Churchill, First Lord of the Admiralty, became alarmed as the Germans were getting closer to capturing many of the channel ports. He surmised that if captured, the ports could be used as bases to attack British shipping. He developed a plan and traveled in late September to France to arrange a transfer of the BEF to the north. Consequently, by October 10, all but one corps had reached the staging area in Saint-Omer-Hazebrouck.

The transfer of troops went undetected by the Germans until October 8. By then it was too late for them to assemble enough troops to confront the British.

October 12th

Today is my wedding anniversary and I am consumed with thoughts of my dear wife and child, which mean more to me than the scrap we are involved in.

In the evening I had a long talk with Lt. Marshall on his thoughts about the duration of the war. He thought it would last until about Christmas.

October 13th -16th

I went with two sections of our guns to a position on Beaulne Ridge. We arrived there about midnight in pitch black darkness. It was heavy going and we could not use lights or even have a smoke because of our close proximity to the enemy.

We got into position without mishap. At dawn the next morning was a sight that was almost indescribable. One could not walk for three yards without stepping in a great shell hole, yet somehow we missed them while setting up the guns.

From the size and number of holes we figured that the guns we were relieving had a terrible time of it. Because of the holes we named this place "Pepper Hill" and the infantry called it "The Devil's Own."

Collins and I worked like slaves digging a small cavity under the riverbank. When we were done it felt quite at home. We talked for a while remembering the good times we had with George Bramwell. I wondered how any of us could tell George's love ones how he died.

October 14th – 16th

When we were not firing our guns; we were like rabbits hiding in our dugout. We remained in this position until the night of the 16th.

While we were leaving a horrific night attack was in progress. We were relieved by the French and we marched all night. We stopped and rested for a few hours, yet by morning we had marched to Neuilly-Saint-Front. From there we continued our advance towards an unknown destination. Although we didn't know where we were headed, we all felt a great relief just to be away from the ceaseless sounds of battle.

October 17th–18th

We traveled by train through Amiens, Boulogne, Calais, and detrained at Hazebrouck, which was 25 miles from the Belgium border. This is where we bivouacked for the night.

October 19th

After marching to Cassel we had a day's rest. During the march my charger had a severe choke. He came down with me on him; but I managed to help him up.

When we arrived in Cassel we were greatly elated to be in a town and feasted ourselves on cakes and sweets. After the hardships of the previous weeks, this was a grand change indeed.

Return to Belgium

After The Battle of Anise, Winston Churchill pulled the BEF and sent them to Hazebrouck, France. From France they marched through villages on their way to Ypres, Belgium. Churchill wanted to prevent the Germans from taking the port cities.

CHAPTER FIVE:

THE FIRST BATTLE OF YPRES

The British wanted to prevent the German forces from occupying the channel ports of Boulogne-sur-Mer and Calais. The city of Ypres was the Germans' last major obstacle and the BEF were determined to prevent them from accomplishing their goal. During the first battle of Ypres both Allied and German forces suffered enormous losses. The British experienced the near destruction of their highly trained and knowledgeable regular army, aptly nicknamed "The Old Contemptibles". The Germans endured heavy casualties among both their young, inexperienced soldiers as well as the highly trained reserves. Despite these significant outcomes, the battle will remain notable in the annals of military history, because it marked the end of mobile operations and the start of trench warfare.

Prior to the arrival of the German Army, the Allies created trench defensive positions around Ypres in the shape of a small salient.[7] The British army held a thirty-five-mile-long line in the center of the bulge, while the French Army protected the British flank south of the city.

On October 20 the German Army Chief of Staff, Falkenhayn, ordered his army to break through the Allied lines and capture the ports of Dunkirk, Calais, and Boulogne. Initially they struck the Belgian defenses on the Yser River near Nieuport. The Belgian forces were unable to hold their positions against the enemy. To prevent the Germans from

---

7   Salient: The trench system projecting toward the enemy.

bypassing Ypres, the Belgians opened the sluice gates and flooded the surrounding land. The Germans were compelled to reconsider their plans, opting to launch a series of attacks against the city of Ypres. As was the case in previous battles, the German forces outnumbered the British until some of the Commonwealth's Indian divisions arrived to replace the reserves.

On October 31 the Germans attacked the British lines along a narrow front on the Messines Ridge, forcing the British troops from their position. The enemy continued advancing until General Haig's First Corps staged a ferocious counterattack.

The German Army continued their mission to break through the British line, but whenever this was accomplished, a British counterattack would drive it back to its prior position.

It wasn't until the onset of winter weather that there was a break in the fighting. The combat had been so unrelenting, and the loss of life so horrific, that the British survivors were content to say that a man was not a soldier unless he had served on the Ypres front. Of the one-hundred and sixty thousand men sent to France with the BEF, thirty percent were either killed in action or died of their wounds. Nevertheless, ninety percent of them were impacted by the encounter in some way, with either physical injuries or some form of mental and/or emotional distress.

First battle of Ypres

October 20th

The battery marched to the city of Poperinghe and once again we were in Belgium. It was an awful sight to see all of the refugees streaming into Poperinghe from the outlying towns and villages; they were trying to keep ahead of the rapidly advancing enemy. I happened to stop to pat a pretty little child on her head and gave her some biscuits that I had in my pocket. The poor little mite was simply starving. Within a minute I was surrounded by starving children. I emptied my pockets and haversack. Then, with a couple of chums, we collected all the biscuits and Bully Beef in the battery and gave them to the women and children.

It was pitiful to see the children struggling to get at us. It was even a harder job to keep away the hungry Belgian men because we didn't have anything for them. We had given the women and kiddies everything we had in the food line. That night we bivouacked outside the town.

October 21st

Before dawn we marched towards the village of Langemarke. As we approached the village it was being heavily shelled.

I, and a couple of others, reconnoitered the area for some time, and failed to find a good position for an observation post. Finally two gun sections took up positions in the rear of the church.

I went with the remaining section through the village. As we passed we saw lots of wounded French soldiers in the open by the churchyard. My section dropped into action by the railway, and again, we attempted to find an observation station. I stopped by a deserted powerhouse that I thought could be used. Later I, along with the remaining battery staff, were ordered to regain the two sections at the rear of the church.

As we went towards the railway crossing, a shell burst in the center of the road, about 30 or 40 yards ahead of us. This all occurred as we galloped past the church wall. Fortunately the shrapnel struck the wall, otherwise it would have been right among us.

I galloped past the spot where I had seen the wounded Frenchmen just two hours before. The whole lot was dead and in pieces. It was a horrible sight.

We rejoined the guns without mishap. George Millington and I were ordered to lay our wire to a large deserted convent near our infantry. As we ran the wire we were sniped at pretty hard by Germans hidden in houses to our left; one missed me by inches. The next morning I went back to the spot, found the bullet, and saved it as a souvenir.

In the afternoon the French infantry had been forced to re-tire; our infantry went up to hold what the French had lost. Although they were greatly outnumbered, they held.

We were firing at very short range, even though we knew we would be observed by the enemy.

The night passed quickly. We were dug in by the side of a stream, which effactually screened us from the continual pres-ence of rifle bullets. We had to go without food all day and were not pleased with the events.

October 22nd

George and I laid our wire to the convent. We described it as heavenly, for it was well-stocked with provisions. We found biscuits, butter, and jam, George and I had a good feast and brought some away with us for the battery.

It got pretty warm getting back to the guns. The enemy sniped at us across a large scarred field.

While waiting for us to set up good communications, two signalers dug a shallow trench by the edge of the field. They amused themselves by putting their hats on a flagpole, raising them until the crown of the hat was just above the crest of the trench. Tempting the Germans to shoot at them proved to be an amusing diversion.

We fired hard all morning. The enemy replying on the village did grand shooting on the church, where shell after shell passed through the steeple. Finally the church caught fire and was soon one mass of flames. The clock steeple collapsed with a crash; it was a dramatic sight. It seemed that they wanted to get at our battery for they shelled the fellows in front and behind our wagon line, wounding a few men and killing some horses.

Fortunately for those of us at the guns, only a few men were wounded. Our infantry was forced to retire, so we requested an infantry escort of 100 men for our guns. All they could send us was one platoon of 20 men.

At dark, George Millington ("Old George") had gone along the wire to forage for food. While he was gone bullets were very plentiful. Eight of us clutched to our little trench, waiting for him to get into communication and return with the spoils.

Things seemed to quiet down for about half an hour when suddenly the Germans played a machine gun dead on us. We thought they had us. Although we did not know it, the infantry was on our left. They had moved while we were waiting for George.

As the infantry took care of the machine gun, I heard strange rustling sounds in the bushes on the other side of the stream. For a moment I thought it was some of the German snipers getting in our rear. I crawled very cautiously on my hands and knees along the stream to a small bridge crossing. I found after no little time that the sound I had heard was caused by some rabbits that our chaps released from an adjoining farm. It was amusing to think about it afterwards but not at the time.

Old George returned, loaded with goods. When I mentioned the machine gun and the rabbit stalking he said, "Blast the guns and rabbits, and have a bit of this strawberry jam, Old China. It's the goods." I declined the food for I was too dry to eat.

Nothing drinkable was to be had except the water in the stream and that was dirty. The rest of the night passed rather quietly. In the morning, out of desperation, I was compelled to drink some of the stream water.

October 23rd–24th

At dawn Old George and I went along our line which was broken during the night. We found some small houses by the road, which had been occupied by some of our chaps the previous day. Surprisingly now they were utterly destroyed.

There was one great hole in the center of the road - one of the largest I had seen. I figured it must have been caused by a very large shell. I recalled the horrific burst in the village where one shell sent a complete house into the air. This must have been the same type of shell.

After mending the breaks in the line, George and I reached a convent and connected the telephone in the attic. On our way back we had to get in a ditch for the shelling was rather hot.

We made it back to the guns and fired a few rounds before the wire was broken again by a coal-box. It was too dangerous to go back out and try to find the break, so we kept up communications using signaling flags.

When things quieted down Old George and I went out and repaired the break. During the morning the wire was broken no less than five times. It was very unhealthy work to find and repair each break.

A little ways to the right of our position was a small farm that had chickens, rabbits, and other provisions in the house. It had been left by the inhabitants, which meant that they were forced to leave in a hurry.

Along with the other animals we found a few goats which we collared. I was content listening to the milk splashing into my pail. I looked up to see how George was progressing. He had a puzzled look on his face, as he attempted to find udders on a billy goat. I had a good laugh about that one! We had our fill then returned to the battery with the remaining goat's milk and provisions.

Later I prevailed upon Old George to slip over to the farm to make a can of tea and bring it back, while I attended to the firing. No sooner had he left than a German horse artillery battery opened dead range upon us and kept up a hot fire for a period of time.

The shelling was so terrible that nothing could have lived above the ground. We were absolutely tied to our little trenches, making it impossible for us to return fire.

The shelling went on for two hours. All I could think about was Old George and how he must have been caught by the shelling on his way to the farm. I was greatly surprised to see him crawling along the trenches with the can in his hand.

While George made his way along the trenches, three guys and two officers, one of whom was Lt. Marshall, stood up and shouted at George to get under cover.

I was also yelling at George at the same time as Lt. Marshall, when I heard a whining and a bang. Lt. Marshall collapsed with seven shrapnel bullets in him; all this happened in a flash.

Old George must have had a charmed life, being able to get to and back from the farm through all of the shelling and live through it. To me it was marvelous.

Even though Lt. Marshall was wounded, George and I drank the tea for it cost near one life and a dozen very narrow escapes. The tea was even better when we added the goat's milk I had procured earlier.

We were shelled heavily all day and several of our men were wounded. Along with them our wagon line and the hospital in our rear caught it.

Our position was undefendable so we received orders to retire at nightfall. At dusk George and I resolved to wind in our wire because we would need it later. New wire was not attainable.

I had just started to pull in the wire when a Johnson burst immediately in front of me, and rather more close than they had usually been.

I immediately laid down while splinters and lumps of earth passed over my head. I remembered that the shells were bursting all day in salvos of four. So I jumped up when I heard the other three shells coming and ran behind a large tree by the stream. In my haste I fell into the stream, which perhaps was well for me to have fallen, for the splinters from the shells took large pieces out of the tree.

We waited for a while. It seemed that the last three shells were the Germans final salvo. So George and I started again and an occasional bullet was all that passed by us on our way to the convent.

It was dark when we got to the convent and pulled the rest of the wire. We hurried down to the crossroads where I instructed a fellow named Hodge to meet us with our horses.

We were held up by some French Cavalry, but eventually we got to where our horses should have been — only to find that Hodge and the horses were not there. We decided to go and look for him.

On the way we heard him coming down the road. George and I hastily decided to give him a scare. We turned our hats with the peaks to the rear and waited. It was very dark when he got near us. We both jumped out near the head of his horse. Old Hodge thought Germans had him and it was not until we burst out laughing that he recognized who we were.

The three of us rode back and rejoined the Brigade as it was marching. We marched through various villages and finally bivouacked about 12 miles from our recent hard scrap. It was great relief to sleep on straw above the damp ground.

October 25th

The Brigade decided to take a day of rest, so we remained at our bivouac site. This farm was inhabited and the owners kindly gave us some of their food.

So we had a feast of bacon and tomatoes, as well as some boiled milk, which was the first cow's milk I've had since I left home. It was a busy morning overhauling phones. In the afternoon I wrote letters.

That night George and I made our beds on some dry straw. Unfortunately it rained hard all night and by morning the straw was near washed away. Without shelter I was wet through.

October 26th–30th

We marched and took a position of readiness at Houghe, which was about 3 miles from Ypres. All was quiet except for an occasional shell.

Our position was located on the grounds of what was once a beautiful chateau, but everything was wrecked and the ornamental lakes and gardens were being used for the horses.

October 28th

On the night of the 28th a shrapnel shell burst over us. The flash and bursting of the shell woke me up. Some of the chaps ran into the woods for shelter, but George and I decided to remain where we were. We soon fell asleep again.

At daylight we found two chaps were wounded, one officer dead, and five horses were killed, while several others were injured. All this took place within 20 yards of where we laid.

October 29th

In the afternoon of the 29th we went into action. Old George and I ran wire. When I went to connect up I was surprised to find a shrapnel bullet embedded in my telephone, which had been by my side the previous night. I fixed it and managed to continue using it.

The battery fired a few rounds and then returned to the chateau where we remained until the morning of the 31st. There was heavy firing all around and a ceaseless stream of infantry wounded going towards Ypres. The weather was horribly wet and the nights very cold.

October 31st–November 6th

We marched through the beautiful old town of Ypres, which contained some very fine buildings, notably the Cloth Hall and Cathedral.

We took up a position of readiness outside the fortification of the town. We dropped into action in various places but did little firing.

The enemy commenced bombarding the town on November 2nd with 17" Howitzers. The noise of the shells passing over our heads was almost indescribable.

On November 5th a few of us got together in the morning and made one of our famous "Bully Stews". We were about to commence the feast when we heard some of the monster shells coming. They fell in the fields on our right and rear so we had to move. As we were moving we heard more coming; they dropped almost in the same place. One shell burst near a cow and threw it bodily about 30 yards.

Then we heard the deafening whistle of one shell that sounded like it was coming directly for us. It reminded me of an express train roaring through the air. We crouched behind one of the ammunition wagons. The shell landed about 15 yards away, exactly on line with our front trench. The concussion from the explosion was horrendous. The wagon rocked as if it were near a minimum earthquake.

Afterwards we measured the gigantic hole. Later that afternoon I found out that the shells were 11.2 inch and not the 17 inch shells we thought they were. However they were three to four times as big again as the often met "Jack Johnsons."[8]

The battery moved by the river. Although the water was very cold I had a plunge and a wash, which was the first since the time of the retreat. It's a very common thing to go a week or even more without having a wash.

At least now food is a little more plentiful. The weather is very wet and the whole country is a veritable sea of mud. The enemy seems to shell everywhere-haphazardly, and especially at night.

---

8   **Jack Johnson:** The nickname given to a German artillery shell. It was named after the boxer Jack Johnson because it was very powerful and really packed a punch.

On the morning of the 6th we were read an appeal from Sir John French urging us to hold on, despite the overwhelming masses of the enemy. We were to continue to prevail until reinforcements could be brought up.

Enemy attacks were twice daily. These, along with the nightly occurrences, made our losses very great. Despite the fact that our trenches were being so thinly manned and our guns so few, our line was formed and maintained.

Thanks to the splendid leadership of our little army and our chaps' love for dangerous scraps, the enemy had been stopped in France as well as in Belgium. We are also grateful for our splendid infantry in the trenches. They suffered infinitely more and in a greater degree, than we did.

November 7th–12th

The battery was assigned to the HQ 25th Brigade for three days. The battery returned each night to a field off of the main road. Things were very quiet except for an occasional shelling.

On the night of the 10th, I waited at the 25th Brigade for my horse to be brought over. After some time George came and told me that it was impossible to bring over horses. He suggested we walk over to them instead. We started out on foot to find our battery. After traveling some good way we knew we were lost.

It was very dark and the road was being shelled. We came upon what seemed to be a deserted farm. We discovered it was occupied by some of our infantry and decided to anchor there till morning. They gave us food and hot tea. Then we placed our blankets on some straw from a stack of hay. This was the best bed we had for some time.

The next morning we were relieved to find our battery. There had been the usual speculation, as well as a few wagers, as to whether or not we had gotten nipped.

On the night of the 12th we came through the most severe storm I have ever experienced. Without a cap I was blinded by the force of the rain and wind. We all looked like drowned rats. It was an awful march in the pitch darkness and blinding rain. I simply held on to the saddle and let my old charger follow the rest.

We were too uncomfortable to sleep in the cold rain and mud. After a great deal of scrounging, George, Collins, and I got into a deserted establishment, and remained there till morning. It was a miserable night. The shelter we got was acceptable, but it took me two days to get dry. I would have given a great deal to have sat before a fire in dry clothes.

November 10th

One section of the battery found action near Zonnebeke. I went with the other two sections to a position by a small wood, about 3 or 4 miles NE of Ypres. We did a little firing.

Towards evening I ran a line to K battery of the Royal Horse Artillery (RHA) to get into communication with the trenches. It was wet and everywhere was bog and mud.

The CO of K Battery and I were standing beside a railway embankment. He was giving it to me hot about the troubles he was having with communications. That didn't set with me well. He and I had high words about the subject, to where he promised to give me 5 years or have me shot. At that point I told him to get on with it, etc. He and I parted before things got out of hand. When I saw him the next morning he treated me quite differently.

That night it rained again so everything was drenched. Because I couldn't find a dry spot to lie down, I had a wet "standing up sleep" by the railway embankment.

November 14th

I went with Left Section to a position beside the 51st battery. They were located on a ridge a thousand yards to the rear of the trenches. From this location we could see the Germans firing from their trench and watch our own lyddite[9] bursting near the enemy's position.

We had hardly begun to fire when they had us spotted. The Prussian Guard made a big attack and our guns, with the 51st, did great slaughter. The ground in front of the trenches was covered with dead Germans along with many of our own chaps.

During the morning they peppered us but we kept on replying. The 51st, with the quick-firing 18 pounders, did grand work keeping up a wall of fire on the Germans' foremost trench.

Early in the afternoon we had to desert our guns. The shelling was so hot it would have been suicide to stay. We took cover in some of the small trenches we dug about 30 yards behind the guns.

About every twenty minutes we would jump out of the trenches and run up to the guns. We would shoot off a couple of rounds then run back to cover. The new 18 pound guns of the 51st were so fast that the crews could rush up and let go six rounds in grand style before the men ran back to cover.

I was with the 51st for two days of training on how to fire the new 18 pound guns. During the two days I was without a drink of any description. My thirst was troubling me more than the shells and bullets.

---

9   **Lyddite:** British explosive used for filling artillery shells in World War One. Actually molten and cast picric acid.

On one occasion, while I was running back from the guns, I came across the officer's cook. He was in a dugout that was about 50 yards to the rear of the guns. I asked him if the officer had water he could spare. The cook gave me a mug of rather dirty-looking water but it tasted grand.

I went back to the 40th Battery with the Sergeant Major of the 51st. While getting there a shell dropped within 10 yards of us. The concussion rather shook us and we immediately fell down to dodge the splinters. On getting up we were both surprised to find that the other was not hurt. I was fortunate, for the shell had cut down a tree that fell across my overcoat which was lying close beside me.

We kept up firing until dark. George, Collins, and I were standing beside a wagon getting something to eat when the enemy's infantry attacked. Their rifle bullets rained down on us as we ran to the gun for shelter behind its shield.

Collins pushed me a little aside. A few seconds later he got a bullet in the foot. Luckily the thickness of his boot diverted the bullet's course. Had he not pushed me I should have caught it, and perhaps not with such lucky results.

After a while George and I managed to get into a small trench that he had dug during the day. The attack dropped off, but they shelled us throughout the night. Although it was cold and wet, we had a good sleep because we were severely exhausted.

In the morning the ground all around was peppered with shell holes. We were indeed thankful that one did not drop into our little trench for quite a few had fallen very near.

November 15th

The section commenced firing during the morning. In return we were shelled a little, but it was nothing in comparison with the previous day.

I went over to the 51st battery to get my telephone, which I had left it in a dugout the day we were receiving new gun instructions. Upon arriving, I found it was occupied by two other telephonists. I heard the sound of an incoming shell and the three of us ran for it. The shell dropped plumb into the dugout and destroyed the instruments. Having fled, we undoubtedly avoided the fate of our instruments.

I returned to my section, and was told that we had orders to take up a position further on the right. The 51st battery remained in its position and had it as bad as, or worse than, the previous day. Two of their guns were put out of action, and the casualties were heavy. One shell killed five men. While they were being buried another shell dropped among the burial party, killing four more.

We reached our right section in the afternoon. I remained with the wagon line on guard duty. It was very wet and cold. Making matters worse, the enemy continued shelling us all night.

November 16th

I moved some wagons into an adjacent wood for airplane cover. While doing so I noticed a ruined farm nearby. I walked over to it. As I passed along the wooden fence a bullet hit a nearby wooden gatepost. I dodged behind the post fearing a sniper had me in his sight. It must have been a spare bullet for nothing else came near me.

During my look around the farm I got a tin of "Bully Beef" in order to prepare a dinner, which I had not had for a considerable time. I had just got it nicely on the go when I was ordered to run a line to the reserve trenches of the Gordon Highlanders. With George's help we reached the trench, where I remained, while George returned to the battery.

Since I didn't bring an instrument with me, I had to borrow one from a Sergeant of the Royal Engineers.

Walking through the trench I reached a dugout, where a Gordon Highlander named Bruce helped me setup communications. (I learned afterwards that Bruce was a famous runner). He warned me to keep low because snipers were active. Almost as he spoke, a fellow coming towards me got a bullet in the chest. The bullet just missed me so I took Bruce's warning and kept low.

It was terribly cold. Bruce asked if I was hungry; he gave me some bread and cheese which I gratefully took.

I sent orders to the guns until after midnight, when things seem to calm down. It was getting so cold at night that I pitied Bruce in his kilt with bare legs. However, he slept sound while I could not sleep a minute. I was glad when morning came. Although I was stiff from the cold, I got up and decided to run up and down the trench for a few minutes. I needed to warm myself, even though I was daring the snipers to hit me.

November 17th

I was still with the 51st battery under the direction of Major Baird of the Gordon Highlanders. He had me send the orders for our guns to cover the trenches as much as possible. Shortly after dawn the enemy made a forceful attack. Considering the small number of men in the trenches, it was marvelous that the enemy didn't break through. About 9:00 a.m. they started to shell us.

The first shell went into a dugout a few yards in front of me and killed a Lt. Colonel as well as his servant. Another shell fell 10 yards to my right and buried Bobby Glue and 3 officers.

We ran over to the dugout and tried to dig them out. Uncovering the officers we discovered that they were either killed or wounded. I was frantically digging, when I found Bobby's lower torso. I tried to pull him out, but his legs had separated from his upper body. This presented an agonizing sight that I shall not forget. Many men were wounded during the first few minutes of this attack.

With the death of Bobby Glue, Fred realized that only he and Pudgie Taylor were left to keep the promise the four of them had made before the battle of Mons. It seemed like an eternity had passed since then, yet it had only been three months. With a heavy heart, Fred slowly walked to the communication dugout to continue his work with the 51st Battery.

November. 17th (continued)

An artillery officer and a man that I didn't recognize rode into our battery position. Upon dismounting, the officer rushed off to find the commander, while the man hitched the two horses to a tree about a yard from my dugout.

Almost immediately afterwards the familiar whine of an incoming shell sent the man jumping into my dugout. The instant he landed inside, a shell burst right over us and killed the two horses. One fell dead right on top of the dugout. Its blood started to flow inside. There wasn't anything we could do but move to a spot in the dugout away from the incoming blood.

The shells were falling like rain with such horrific force that they caused all the Gordons to run for it. The shelling was so murderous that I also felt like running. However, I realized that if I left my instrument that our guns would not be able to return fire. I stuck while the Gordons ran, all except Bruce. He asked me if I was going to stay and I said yes. He replied, "If it's good enough for you, it's good enough for me."

As one chap was running past us a shell exploded, sending a splinter deep into his leg and a bullet in his arm. I dragged him into the dugout and Bruce and I bandaged him up. He stayed with us throughout the day.

Two more attacks took place and every available man was pressed forward, which amounted to very few.

During the day Bruce was telling me that of the 1400 in his regiment that left Plymouth in September, all that remained were he and 34 others. He went on to say that they had had some horrible times but this was worse than any of them. I fully believed him, for I also was sick of being shelled and tired of the smell of gunpowder and blood.

Whenever I received information from our observation post I would write a note. Bruce would run it to Major Baird's location and return with the Major's order for the guns. All day the enemy kept up the fierce bombardment. That night when Old George came to relieve me, I was fairly done in. Having experienced Bobby's death I felt sick. On top of that I hadn't had any sleep and very little food for four nights.

When I reached our guns, Collins took on the instrument while I wrapped myself up in my two wet blankets. Even though it was freezing cold and snow started to fall I slept like a top. The next morning I felt a little better, so I was quite able to carry on with the business.

November 18th–21st

I remained with our guns while George stayed with the Gordons. We did considerable firing and occasionally an enemy shell would pass over. It was peace when compared with the previous day. We were informed that we were to be relieved by the French. Therefore we could withdraw from the battle for a rest, as well as to be refit with more horses and men.

When the battery was assembled, I was also told that our center section had a warm time of it. Hodges, my lube-off man, was killed. Farmer along with several others were wounded.

We were overjoyed at the idea of a rest. A change from the ceaseless scrapping of the past few weeks would be very welcomed.

November 22nd

We left our position at dawn and marched to Ypres. On the way I couldn't help but notice that the whole countryside was in a horrible condition. Not a building was standing, either on the farms or in the town itself. All of the beautiful buildings were destroyed. I thought of how different it was when we marched through the town less than a month before.

The battery marched safely through the town. All day we continued to march forwards through the cold.

My old charger had a hard time keeping his legs under him because the roads were slippery. So I walked most of the time.

It was dark when we arrived at a farm located a few miles from Merris and billeted there for the night. How strange it seemed to me to be away from the ceaseless roar of gunfire, etc., and be transported to the peace and quiet of a farm where the sheds, barns, and cow houses seemed like mansions. It was a blessing to be able to sleep in a building and off of the miserably wet, cold ground.

November 22nd–December 12th

Our period of rest was greatly appreciated for a time, but soon it became monotonous.

Some of our officers received short leaves. Through the good graces of Major Madocks I was given a 48 hour pass to Boulogne.

The Major took his leave in England. When he arrived he was kind enough to give my dear wife instructions on how to get to Boulogne in time to meet me. I left camp on the evening of the 1st of December, and rode into Hazebrouck to catch the train to Boulogne. My wife's train was scheduled to leave at 7:00 a.m. the next morning, therefore I was expecting to meet her at 5:00 p.m. I didn't know that she had arrived earlier, so I was delighted when we met at 11:00 a.m. instead.

Our stay together was about the shortest 28 hours of my life. To leave her the next day was the hardest thing I had experienced through the whole campaign. It was a very sad train ride back to Hazebrouck. All I could think about was how grand it was to hold my dear wife, to be someplace peaceful and safe, and to take in the smell of clean linens instead of the stench of rotting flesh.

Upon arriving at camp the next day, I immediately noticed that all the men were getting impatient to get back to the business of ending this war. We were all pleased to hear that on the 11th of December we were heading back to the firing line

December 13th

We marched to Pon de Neippe and billeted in a farm just outside the village. In the distance we could hear the old familiar sounds of artillery fire and rockets deployed from the trenches.

December 14th

We marched through Ploegstrestte and chose a location beside the 35th Battery, positioned in what was once a beautiful garden behind an old chateau.

George and I ran our line beyond the chateau to some ruined houses. From there we had a good view of the German trenches and beyond to the town of Messines.

On my way back to the battery I found a partly destroyed house and went inside. I was surprised to find a young woman and her five little children, along with the woman's brother. She told me that her husband was a soldier who had been killed and the house was all she had left.

The baby reminded me of my own baby daughter, so I asked if I could take the baby from its bed and hold her. The woman agreed and gave me some hot milk to feed to the baby.

Before leaving I tried my best to induce her to leave her house to move to a safer place, but she refused. All I could do was give them my peppermints and all the odd money I had left. On my journey back I was rather upset, thinking about the poor little kiddies. I never had time to go that way again so I don't know the outcome of their circumstance, but I thought about the kiddies often.

Upon my return I met some old chums from the 35th Battery. It was nice to talk over the old soldiering days we spent in the reserves.

December 15th–20th

The battery remained in position for the bombardment of Messines, although we did little firing until the 20th when the actual bombardment started. Our wagon line was shelled out in the morning but fortunately only one man was wounded. However, we lost most of our ammunition. Later in the morning when we were heavily shelled by the Germans we had few shells to return fire vigorously. We remained in position until 5:00 p.m. when we marched back to our rest billet.

December 21st–23rd

The battery remained at the rest billet until the morning of the 23rd, when we marched to Bethune and billeted in a schoolhouse.

We arrived at the schoolhouse as the sun was setting. George and I were unpacking our things when we discovered that in our haste, we had left our blankets at the last billet. The thought of spending another night on an uncomfortably hard surface didn't conjure up warm feelings. We resolved that we were going to find a bed somewhere. Upon leaving the schoolhouse we happened upon a Frenchman. Using our best French, we inquired about lodging. Just as our negotiations were faltering his daughter arrived. She invited us to stay at their home nearby.

When we entered the house we immediately realized that the family was very poor, but they treated us handsomely. The mother was an elderly woman who doted on us. She gave us as much as we could possibly eat and drink. Afterwards she made up a bed on the floor near the fireplace.

Knowing that we had to report back to camp in the morning, she woke us at 3:15 a.m. giving us time to drink some hot coffee before we left. We wanted to pay her for her hospitality but she became indignant and refused.

When we arrived back at camp at 4:20 a.m., the battery was preparing to march towards La Bassee where we were to take up a position.

December 24th

We arrived at Cambrai, where we established our position with the towns of Cuinchy and Givenchy on our left. Each town was in a state of ruin from the heavy scrapping that had recently taken place.

George and I were very busy firing up our communications after taking over the wires of the 47th Battery. We had a grand observing station that was in the ruins of a brewery. It was beautifully furnished at one time but now everything was destroyed, including the lovely carved furniture, ornaments, a piano, and a large gramophone. Everything had been left where it stood. I went into the kitchen and secured a few plates, cups, and an assortment of cooking utensils that I took back to the guns.

Late that night I was ordered to get into communication with the 2nd Infantry Brigade. This required me to lay down additional wire, an uncomfortable task.

Rifle bullets kicked up dirt as they fell around me. However, I did the job without mishap and got back to my dugout.

It was Christmas Eve and my thoughts were far away, recalling Christmas Eves of the past. Sadness and loneliness overcame me and I went to bed with a heavy heart.

December 25th

I forgot it was Christmas Day even though I remembered last night being Christmas Eve. Perhaps I intentionally forgot it was Christmas Day, not wanting to revisit the sadness of the night before.

For whatever reason, I kept busy firing up communications the entire day. I was so busy that I didn't notice how quiet it was. Then some of the chaps got together to fix a Christmas dinner.

It suddenly came to me why it was so quiet. A mutual truce was declared in order to celebrate Christmas. One of our chaps secured a chicken and some vegetables to make a Christmas feast.

George came down from the observing station and together, along with a couple of other chaps, we went to a large house nearby. We collared a piano and brought it back to the guns. One of the chaps played Christmas carols. It wasn't a great success but we made the best of it, for we knew there were many poor devils that were worse off than us.

December 26th

It was a rather quiet day with only an occasional shelling. I took this opportunity to warm some water for a wash. I was sorely in need of a wash since it would be the first I had in four days. The battery did a little firing during the day.

It had been raining and our dugout was swamped, so we moved into a small shed that was located at the rear of the farm. The day was very cold with drizzling rain that continued throughout the day.

December 27th–28th

Nothing unusual happened today, except we fired in intervals at German working parties. Meanwhile, the German artillery searched all over for our gun placement. Every now and again they fired a shell, but nothing came near us.

Throughout the night we kept up a very slow rate of fire with long intervals between salvos, making it difficult for the enemy to locate our position.

I've been on duty day and night with the phones, but I'm used to it now and it takes little or no effect. Just the same, I'm exhausted from the lack of sleep for I never have a complete night's rest.

December 29th–30th

The battery did a lot of firing today and we were credited with smacking up a German field battery near La Bassee.

December 31st

The morning was rather quiet. At 2:30 in the afternoon we were subjected to a fierce bombardment along with a heavy infantry attack. The enemy captured our central tower, or keep[10], which was located by the railway embankment. They took it from the King's Royal Rifles, although later that afternoon they recaptured it.

Around 10:00 p.m. the Germans attacked and regained the keep, as well as the redoubt[11].

Even though it was very cold our battery was firing heavily all night. At 3:00 a.m., after two counterattacks, we succeeded in retaking the ground we had lost. Unfortunately we couldn't hold it.

The Kings Royal Rifles (KRR) were bombed out soon after they gained possession. Throughout the night we kept up a hot fire until about 8:00 a.m. We brought the New Year in with a real "Bang"!

January 1st

After a long night manning the telephone I was exhausted, so I was delighted to hand over the instruments to Collins.

After leaving the dugout I found a stable to sleep in and slept throughout the day, even through a little shelling that took place.

January 2nd–23rd

During the past 20 days it has been the usual give and take of obtaining small patches of land that cost dearly in human

---

10   **Keep:** a stronghold or the innermost fortified part of a castle.
11   **Redoubt:** a temporary fortification built to defend a position.

lives. Every day we fired at any targets that were presented to us. At night the enemy would return the favor.

The redoubt was taken and lost many times. Each attack resulted in a couple hours of fierce scrapping. Since neither side could hold on to the redoubt, the land between our trenches and the enemy was termed "No Man's Land".

At night the rifle bullets made it rather uncomfortable to sleep. The weather has been very wet and cold; in fact we have even received a few heavy snowstorms.

Many of the men were coming down with fever. Eventually I got a fever high enough that it caused me to vomit in a bucket, but I was still able to carry on with business.

The night attacks were becoming very frequent. We suffered very few casualties except for a few wounded. We lost more men to sickness than from enemy gunfire.

One day during this period I went into Bethune and found a place to take a much needed bath and a change of underclothing. I knew that I was beginning to smell like livestock so taking a wash must have been a relief to my chums.

January 29th

During the day the enemy used their eight-inch Howitzers to bombard the docks on the canal. They also shelled the railway line which was by our observing station. They must have sent over 129 shells but did little material damage. One shell fell plumb on the railway line, flinging about a 4-foot piece of the rail a thousand yards. It sailed right over our guns falling a few yards from where I stood. When I heard it coming through the air I thought it was a shell, so I fell to the ground.

Later I read about the incident in the papers, I smiled to see how much the reporters made of it. When it actually *happened we took little or no notice. We were rather more interested in watching the effect of German fire on the canal lock. Wagers were pending on their ability to hit their target.*

January 25th

The night passed quietly with less than the usual amount of shooting. Around 7:15 a.m. I received a message from the 25th Battery that a German observer was captured. They found out from him that the Germans were planning a big attack on our front at Givenchy and Cuinchy around 7:30 a.m. He also revealed that the attack would be preceded by a heavy bombardment.

I immediately sent a message to our observing station, then hurriedly roused the gun detachments and the officers. When the bombardment started it was more horrific than any of the other ones I experienced. The sound of artillery fire was continuous, except when they fired their 17 inch guns.

The whine of hundreds of shells going through the air, mixed with the explosion of both above and ground level shells, was deafening. All around me great mounds of earth were uplifted by bursting shells.

We rapidly replied with gunfire of our own, which added greatly to the unbearable noise. The smoke from gunfire and bursting shells was so heavy, that at times we couldn't see our target.

The enemy captured our first line of trenches and our infantry fell back towards our observing station. Two out of three of our phone lines were cut by shells. While I attended to the instruments Collins ran a line to the left gun section. During the process Collins got knocked on the knee by a shell fragment. The same shell wounded two men and killed the young officer, Mr. Watkins, who had only joined us 8 days previous.

I sent two of my chaps along the observing line. Soon after they left the line to the 25th Battery was broken. I hastily got Collins, who was limping, to attend to the phones while I went along the line to the 25th to try and locate the break.

We were being heavily shelled, so I was very uncomfortable while following the line and listening to the shrapnel and bullets striking the ground around me. I found a couple of yards of the line that had been cut by shrapnel. The break occurred where the wire went through a vine that ran along the top of a wall. So I climbed up on the wall, but had to drop very quickly when a shell seemed to whiz inches from my head. I noticed that a piece of wire was holding the vine to the wall. I cut the wire and the vine fell, which allowed me to repair the line. I was very glad when I reached the 25th to find that communication was coming through.

I took a while recovering my breath before my return to the 40th Battery. On my way back a shell exploded directly in front of me. I had a very clean shave from one of its splinters, but after that the rest of my journey went without mishap.

I just arrived when another big shell burst right on the farm, about 20 yards from the building where my chum was sitting. Luckily the shell didn't do much damage except to the building.

Then another shell fell right into the shelter where the telephones for the left section were located. It severely wounded one man. All in all I had one horrific morning.

The heavy bombardment forced our infantry to retire. Since our battery position was the foremost battery behind their trenches, I knew if our infantry lost the small ridge in front of us, it would be the finish of us and our guns. We were fortunate that our third line stood, allowing us to keep up firing at near ground level. Our guns performed splendidly, doing great execution among the masses of advancing Germans.

The Guards Brigade, consisting of the London Scottish, Seaforths, Camerons and Royal Guards, were brought up as reinforcements, to stop the German advance. However, the Germans entrenched themselves behind our original line. In spite of all of our attacks, the Germans, with overwhelming odds against them, held on to the ground they had gained.

January 26th

At 7:00 a.m. our battery put down a fierce bombardment that lasted about 3 hours. Then the Guards made a counterattack to try to regain the ground we had lost the day before. They recovered a little but failed to accomplish their main objective - to get back to our original five trenches.

We fired feverishly and were shelled in return, with one 6-inch shell going right into the cellar of the farm close to the battery's left section. Out of all the shells that fell on or near us, only two men were wounded.

The fight went on more or less all day. We failed to get any further forwards, but we did manage to repulse an attack from the Germans.

In the afternoon the 1st Siege Battery, which was positioned to our left rear, got it hot. One shell went right into the farm building where they were in action. It set the building ablaze. I watched the gunners running to and from the burning barn removing the wounded in spite of the heavy shelling.

After a while they managed to put out the fire even through the persistent shelling. It was grand to watch them, although my view was obscured from time to time from the smoke being emitted by both the shells and fire. They stuck to it grandly. After putting out the fire they started shooting again with greater intensity, as if they wanted to inflict great damage on the enemy in retaliation for those that were put out or wounded.

January 27th–28th

After two days of attacks, counterattacks, and very severe scrapping, we regained all the lost ground. A large number of prisoners were taken.

There were no further casualties at the guns, which was lucky considering the shellfire the enemy was putting over us.

The Germans did a great deal of entrenching during the nights which gave us some good targets to shoot at during the day.

Our guns were still working dandy in spite of the enormous amount of shooting they had done throughout the campaign. They remained perfectly accurate which accounted for much of our success.

January 29th–February 5th

We had a rather quiet period with very little interaction with the enemy. There were times when we would fire and they never replied. Our attacks of the previous week seemed to have quieted them considerably.

February 6th

We bombarded the Germans' front line trenches from Brickfield to the Railway Triangle. Our firing was so effective that the Royal Guards advanced and captured the trenches without losing a man. Afterwards our artillery was highly praised in a letter from the field commander for the splendid work we did.

There was special inference given to the way communications were maintained by the telephone operators. Undoubtedly it was meant for our battery. As an example, one time I was receiving and sending firing orders to three other batteries besides our own. We had also quickly repaired all three lines that had been broken by shellfire.

The next day the battery received orders to move and relieve the 56th Battery RFA.

February 7th

On arriving at the 56th I reported to the Captain. Together we proceeded to the town of Croix Barbette. I was ordered to take over the wire and communications for our battery that would be arriving about midday.

One of the telephonists from the 56th took me along their observing wire which ran to the trenches. While it was rather quiet, save for the occasional bullet, the chap with me was rather merry. At one point, because of snipers, he advised me to crawl on my hands and knees across a part of the ground that was just to the rear of the trenches.

I followed his advice for a little ways. But on seeing the Royal Engineer fellow walking about unconcerned, I figured if it's safe enough for him, it is safe enough for me. So I stood up and walked—much to the other fellow's disgust.

Momentarily he got wild when I insisted upon him helping me to mend a broken wire that I had propped up on some trees. Afterwards he angrily crawled back, which was quite unnecessary considering I walked back without anything coming near me. Then he took me along some reserve trenches where a few light shells fell.

He and I traced a wire into a redoubt and quickly dodged inside when a shell whizzed over. There was an infantry telephonist inside the redoubt, who in a rather unconcerned voice stated, "Just in time, mates. Three of ours were put out just outside a few minutes ago." He was working away like he was unaware of the goings on outside the redoubt. So we had a chat for a few minutes before we started back (much to the relief of the chap with me).

Meanwhile the enemy was shelling Richebourg Church with coal-boxes. It caught my fancy. I stood on the road and watched about 20 shells go over, although each failed to reach the church.

At night I went into the village and had a few drinks of rotten trench beer before returning to the 56th.

I found a barn and slept in the loft, getting the best night's unbroken sleep that I have had since we were at rest seven weeks before.

February 8th

I had much of the day on my own to stroll about while waiting for the battery to arrive. The battery reported in about 6:00 p.m., but we couldn't bring them into action until after dusk because of an enemy observation plane flying about.

The 56th Battery moved their position more towards Richebourg. The newly-arrived battery took up their old position which included the farm. It was about the most comfortable billet I had ever had regarding our accommodations.

The farm building had escaped shellfire. This was strange considering that the village located at the back, the left and right of the farm had been "through it".

February 9th–17th

The battery did very little firing during this time. It was the calmest setting we had been in since the war began.

Except Collins having a couple of squeaks while repairing the line, nothing worth reporting happened. During this time not *a shell came near us and we did very little night firing. We called it rest.*

February 18th

The battery was recalled from action to go to rest, which I found quite odd since our current billet was so peaceful. They could have allowed us to stay where we were. Ironically, we had to pack everything up and march some distance in order to rest! We marched via Bethune to rest billet near Lilliers.

I was fortunate in securing a billet in a house occupied by an old lady. She gave me a rather crude bed. Although it was hard, it still was a great change. I was greatly elated in hearing that I should be going on leave during this period.

February 19th–March 2nd

During our period of rest we were still well employed in over-hauling all the equipment. It amused me thinking about the differing definitions of rest. To the army, rest means a rest from war but not from work.

I was to go on leave on March 3rd, but I was bitterly disap-pointed when the order came in that all leaves were stopped from March 1st.

March 3rd

We marched from our rest billet towards Richebourg and bil-leted at night near La Fosse. It was very wet and cold.

George and I went foraging and by using our good French, managed to get a good feast of eggs at a farmhouse nearby.

CHAPTER SIX:

THE BATTLE OF NEUVE CHAPELLE

The Battle of Neuve Chapelle took place between the 10 th and 13 th of March, 1915. Located in northwestern France, Neuve Chapelle is north of La Bassee and west of Lille.

Sir John French's plan was to capture Neuve Chapelle then push forwards to the village at Aubers, situated a mile east of Neuve Chapelle. If he successfully captured Aubers, his army would attack the German defenses at Lille, a major communication hub.

To accomplish these goals Sir John French had amassed 374 pieces of artillery. Douglas Haig's First Corps were to lead the attack after a 35 minute artillery barrage. It was reported that the shelling was so intense, that it resembled machine gun fire.

The focus of the shelling was along the German frontline. The bombardment was so devastating, that when the shelling lifted, only small sections of the enemy's trench remained. All of the entanglements were in ruin, allowing the British to rush through the opening.

Often there was hand-to-hand fighting as the British and Indian infantry made a rapid advance towards Neuve Chapelle. It took just four hours to secure the village. Nevertheless, the artillery barrage around Aubers was lacking in both scope and intensity, thus causing little damage to the enemy's trench entanglements. Of the 1,000 troops that attacked Aubers, no one survived.

Due to the lack of artillery shells, as well as communication problems, the British were unable to maintain the extensive artillery pressure necessary to prevent the enemy from bringing up its reserves. With the accumulated strength of its reserves, the Germans launched a coun-terattack on March 12. The British were able to repel the attack and hold the ground they had gained.

This battle was the first offensive undertaken by the British from static, set-piece trenches, where several military innovations were put into place, including timed lifts of artillery barrages. Other strategies newly employed were: color-coded maps marked with objectives to be taken, a concurrent areoplane bombing sequence, and the maintenance of effective secrecy prior to the bombardment.

Battle of Neuve Chapelle

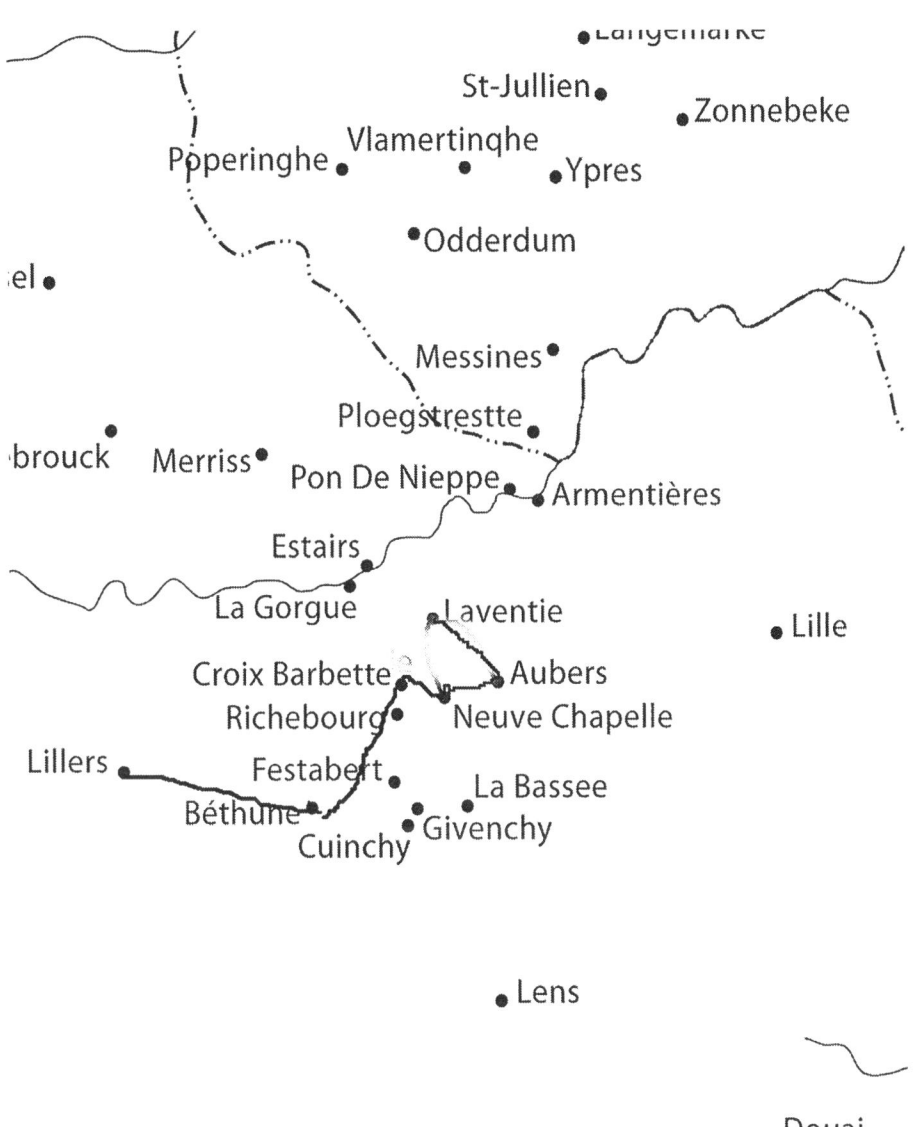

March 4th

We started our march at 3:00 a.m. and came into action about 400 yards on the right of the Richebourg Church.

We were informed that we were to bombard Neuve Chapelle, a village that was on our left front. It had been in the hands of the Germans since October. We took a firing position and then engaged in digging a gun pit and fortifying our position as much as possible.

March 5th–9th

Our battery is preparing for the big bombardment that is to take place in a couple of days. We were joined by several other batteries and soon forces were everywhere. There were guns under almost every tree. Our giant 15 inch Howitzer was to make her debut, as well as quite a few of our new 9.2 inch guns. Communications would be critical so George and I made sure that we laid out double lines to our observing station, as well as lines to various parts of the trenches.

Large amounts of ammunition were distributed at each gun. Every preparation was made to give the Germans the biggest shock they had yet to receive at our hands.

March 10th

The bombardment of Neuve Chapelle commenced at 7:30 a.m. along a four mile front. It was beyond description, listening to the tons of metal going through the air from all 476 guns. Our heavy artillery, a new 18 pound gun, was to concentrate on the enemy's trenches in order to cut the enemy's wire entanglement. All the batteries kept up their fierce rate of firing for three-quarters of an hour. The bombardment was only lifted around the Bois-du-Beiz area to enable our infantry to attack.

Our trenches were lined with Garhwalis[12], Gurkhas[13], and several other regiments of native troops from India. The Leicestershire Regiment made the first charge, capturing the German trenches in grand style. They were held up on the edge of an orchard outside Neuve Chappell until a regiment of Territorials'[14] came to their assistance. With reinforcements a horrific battle of hand-to-hand fighting ensued, especially at a spot that we later called "The Street of Hell".

The massive scale and fierceness of the fighting was more than I can describe. We finally gained control of the village about midday.

While the Leicestershire Regiment made their charge, the natives advanced on the right and captured the trenches in front. However, they were held up by machine guns in a redoubt that was located on the left edge of the Bois du Biez.

The Gurkhas did grand work, especially with their wicked little knives, which accounted for many slit German heads. When the Germans ran from their trenches the little Gurkhas were right after them. Many of the little chaps would climb on the backs of the big Germans and cut their throats in the style of Sweeney Todd.

The Seaforths were brought up to assist. They made a splendid charge, which (according to our officers, and many old campaigners observing with us), was the finest sight they had ever witnessed. The Seaforths went into the murderous machine gunfire as though they were going to a picnic. In spite of the enormous losses they captured the redoubt, along with its contents of Germans and the machine guns. Meanwhile,

---

12   **Garhwali:** a group of people who primarily live in the Garhwal Himalayas of the northern Indian state of Uttarakhand.

13   **Gurkhas:** A regiment of the British and Indian armies comprised of people from Nepal.

14   **Territorials:** Is the spare time volunteer force of the *British* Army

British infantry on our left and beyond the village of Neuve Chapelle had dug themselves in, in front of the Bois du Biez.

During the afternoon the enemy launched several massive counterattacks inflicting heavy losses on our troops. However, our infantry did not budge an inch. We didn't lose any of the ground we had gained.

After witnessing how my observing line had maintained communications throughout the day, contributing to the accuracy of our artillery, the Major credited us with doing good work. Not including shrapnel rounds, we launched 1201 rounds of lyddite, making it a fierce day of firing.

We maintained a constant fire until dark, at which time we slowed down and searched for enemy reinforcements. We were glad when darkness came for it gave us a little respite.

Strange as it seemed, considering our heavy losses, we were a happy crowd that night. The feeling of jubilation was especially true for our battery staff. Even though the day's horrors were not forgotten, we rejoiced in the thought that we had given the enemy a little taste of the gruel that they so often gave to us. We had easily beaten them at their own game. As tired as I was this night, I managed to write my usual letter to my little girl.

March 12th

In the light of the next day, we could see how our infantry had suffered horribly in return for the ground they gained. We were dismayed by the countless streams of wounded that were coming from the front.

From our observation post we could see the ground between our old and new line of trenches, covered with corpses of both our chaps and those of the Germans. This was especially true in Neuve Chapelle.

We immediately opened fire on the Bois Du Beiz, which was still held by the enemy. We learned that the 7th division had advanced as far as possible on our left, but had failed to take Aubers Ridge.

In an effort to coordinate our division our commander was ordered to consolidate the position we had won and hold it. We did this in spite of numerous German counterattacks.

It was awful to see the Germans mowed down by our guns, for they made attack after attack in close formation and were literally blown to pieces. Every attack caused the ground in front of our trenches to grow thicker with bodies. A column of their reinforcements were caught plumb by our 15 inch Howitzer. One round made a gap in the column of about 60 yards. Men, horses, and vehicles were gone into thin air, resulting in mass confusion amongst the enemy.

My phone line, marvel of marvels, still held only being broken once by shellfire. The day was much the same as yesterday with continual firing and streams of wounded and prisoners. As one batch of enemy prisoners made their way through the Rue-du-Bois, three of their own shells came banging into them, killing or wounding about 20 prisoners. What was strange was the shells never touched any of the natives who were escorting them. Our artillery observers in the vicinity thought it was funny to see the natives laughing at the Germans, because they were being ousted by their own chaps. This seemed to amuse them greatly - so much so that they made the Germans walk slowly and keep to the road. It was evident the scared prisoners would have liked to have run across country.

March 13th

The battery kept up a steady rate of fire throughout the night, raising a little at dawn and throughout the morning.

We engaged various targets until the enemy commenced to bombard Richebourg, about 400 yards to our left.

They were using salvos from the 8.2 Howitzers (nicknamed "coal-boxes" or "Jack Johnsons").

In the afternoon my communication broke down. Consequently the battery had to stop firing.

Whilst along the line crossing a main road, shells were falling pretty thick. Nevertheless, the majority were landing in the village. Eventually I found the break in the wire, caused by a shell hitting it square, chopping a piece out of it.

To repair the line I jumped into my favorite cover, a hole made by the shell that broke the wire. Following the repair, I tapped in and found everything all right. Soon I discovered another broken line which I repaired. Attaching my phone to the line, I inquired as to who was on the other end. It was the 9th Brigade who profusely thanked me, for it had saved them an uncomfortable job.

The shelling was pretty hot when I reached the Battery, but the guns were very lucky for nothing fell between us and the village. The enemy was fiercely bombarding the poor old church. There we were, two telephonists and I, watching the effect of the fire. We were speculating which would be the next to go in the air. With every salvo several splinters whizzed over our heads. We took no notice until one small piece hit me in the muscle of my right arm. Luckily it did not penetrate.

The next salvo sent a good-sized piece that grazed my cheek, ultimately burying itself about 2 inches into the ground at my feet. After scratching it out of the ground, I thought to myself that if I had been a couple of inches closer it would no doubt have given me a nasty knock.

We realized that we had watched the fun long enough, so we went into our little house and had "tea" and milk, kindly supplied to us by some nearby cows. Nothing short of an earthquake would make us miss our tea time and milk with tea is bon.

In the morning the Manchesters' caught five spies in Richebourg. They were found hiding in an underground cellar and must have been there for months. They received scant ceremony, as I had no doubt they were soon put out of this world quickly. For spies, either men or women, were promptly dealt with — especially by the French.

The night was rather quiet and we did only a little firing. We had gained and consolidated our objectives so the Germans seemed glad to keep things quiet as long as we would allow.

March 14th–15th

Things remained rather quiet so we did little firing. However, Collins had a squeak on the 14th while going along a wire.

A shell burst missed him, but caught a Gurkha square, cutting him clean in two. During this period, I rode my charger into Richebourg to have a look around. I walked all over the deserted town, passing desolated piles of ruins that not long ago had been a pretty little village.

The church had suffered severely, for only parts of the walls and tower were remaining. The churchyard was pitiful to look at because shells had heaved up the graves and tombs, spreading skulls and bones about everywhere. The top of the steeple had been caught fair by a shell and had fallen. It stuck firmly in the ground by the church door almost as if it had been placed there.

Everywhere I looked there was a mass of wreckage that I can hardly describe. One would have to see it for themselves in order to understand the devastation.

March 16th

We marched to Paqault where we billeted until receiving orders to move before dawn on the 17th.

March 17th

Upon arriving at our position near the town of Laventie, the battery dropped into action although the town was partially in ruins already.

George and I were busy all day laying our line to a ruined house located near the rear of our trenches. From the house we could observe the German lines in the town of Aubers.

While laying the line, George and I went into an abandoned establishment that remarkably was still intact. The house was beautifully furnished. In the attic we found an abundance of women's clothes. In the downstairs kitchen I secured plates and cooking utensils, as well as several other things that would be useful, taking them back with us to the guns.

There was a field that surrounded the house containing a good number of graves of our chaps, much like a miniature cemetery. Every grave was fenced, complete with a cross bearing the soldier's name. I thought to myself that perhaps one day it would be consolation for some women to visit the site where their dear one was laid to rest. This idea stayed with me and caused my thoughts to wander far away to my family back in England. These thoughts brought on my unhappy mood for the rest of the day.

That night I slept but little, not because of the bitter cold, but due to thoughts of my dear wife and daughter visiting a plot of earth containing my own remains.

March 18th–April 3rd

The only time we fired our guns was when requested by either the observation post or a reconnaissance airplane.

I found it very interesting using a powerful light to signal information to an observation airplane. It assisted us in focusing in on doing damage to German gun targets. The German observation airplanes were also very active, but our anti-aircraft guns firing 13 pound shells gave them a warm reception.

On the 25th the Germans brought down one of our planes, which crashed into "No Man's Land". We were ordered to destroy the plane with our guns to prevent the enemy from getting any of the remnants.

Enemy planes frequently dropped bombs on the town of Estaires, which was 5 miles from us and Laventie. As in every town and village I've been, the churches have suffered greatly. I don't understand why the enemy selects churches of any kind, especially the beautiful old structures, proceeding to utterly destroy them.

On the 27th of March I rode through the town of Laventie at a stretch gallop for the town was being shelled.

I stopped a little ways outside the town and watched a church catch fire which always seemed to fascinate me. Even though I hated to see churches destroyed, I had to admit that the enemy did some grand shooting. They repeatedly hit the church until one shell cleanly cut off the only remaining pinnacle.

I learned that the 37th battery, including my old 55th battery, were in action near us. After a great deal of scouting I rode my old charger almost up to our infantry's trenches, but I was stopped by sentries and forced back.

I rode around and eventually found them, spending a pleasant afternoon with all of my old comrades, except Sergeant Major and two others who had received commissions and moved on.

Great changes had taken place during the last 3 years. Most of the old officers, except one, were gone. I learned that several of my old chums had been mortally wounded, and I was deeply saddened to hear that one of my old friends, Hayman, was killed. The last time I saw him was on Christmas Eve, 1913, when I was shopping with my dear wife.

I little thought then that the next time I would hear about him would be the news that he was blown to bits. They told me that their battery had been hotly shelled, and when the shelling stopped, they only found his legs with the rest of him in just bits and pieces. Regrettably I also learned that, just two weeks before the war, he had married a girl living in Lombard du Brittersca. Too many women became widowed of late.

On Good Friday George and I were interviewed by our CO. We were told that he was forwarding a strong recommendation for Old George and I to be granted commissions. Afterwards he "heartily" advised us to take the promotions this time and not refuse them as we had previously.

I took several rides on the wagon lines as they passed through Estaires and Laventie. I enjoyed this period of time for it was practically inactive as far as action with the enemy. Only two shells had come near the guns. The bombardment of Aubers was postponed when we received orders to take up old positions at Croix Barbette.

April 4th

Collins and I proceeded to Croix Barbette to take over the wires and communications of the 35th Battery. We arrived about midday, and inspected the wire that went to the observation station. The station was located in what little remained of the brewery in Neuve Chapelle.

As Collins and I traveled along the wire, I found it interesting to scan the ground that we had won in the big scrap on the 10th of March. Everywhere I looked was in hapless ruin. Even the old German trenches were in very battered condition. I could not walk without stepping in a shell hole or on a grave. Many of the graves had been ploughed up by shells and the remains reburied.

There were still scores of dead German bodies lying on the ground between the trenches. It has been almost a month since the end of the battle. The smell of rotting bodies was not pleasant.

The church and churchyard were utterly destroyed, but strangely enough a large crucifix was standing intact, apparently untouched, while everything else within a mile from it had been battered to pieces. In the entire village there was not a house standing, only piles of debris and memories remained.

We were told that one of the lines was broken so Collins and I went along the wire to find and mend the break.

While following the wire, enemy rifle bullets were plentiful. At times we were in full view of the German trenches. However, we fixed up the line without mishap.

On the way back we came across the gear of a telephonist of the 35th who had been killed earlier. We were saddened for we knew him quite well. The worse thing was that he was killed by one of our own 6 inch shells that had fallen short. During this same event another one of our own shells had landed in a field in front of our battery, killing 2 and wounding several others.

Some other batteries had been ordered to remain at this location after our battery had left.

A few of these men reported that it hadn't been as quiet as it was when we were here before. From the devastated sights around us, this was quite evident. Even so, the buildings on the little farm were still intact.

All the inhabitants at the rear of the village had been cleared out. I walked around the deserted streets. In what was left of one house I found a woolen mattress. This made a grand bed, much preferable to the straw ones I had been using. The mattress was firm and warm, even when it was wet.

Our battery came in rather late. Although things seemed a little loud in front, it was only a "wind" attack. The batteries at our rear fired slowly all night.

CHAPTER SEVEN

THE SECOND BATTLE OF YPRES

The Second Battle of Ypres could be considered as a resumption of the first battle, since weather conditions and the coming of winter had curtailed the continuation of fighting. Although sporadic fighting continued throughout the winter, neither side launched a major offensive.

The German Army was planning a major attack when the weather improved in April. This would be the only major German offensive on the Western Front in 1915. Some historians believe that the primary reason for this offensive was to distract the Allied army's attention away from the Eastern Front.

Perhaps the Second Battle of Ypres is best remembered for the introduction of the German Army's newest weapon, chlorine gas, than for any strategic achievements. Chlorine gas is heavier than air, so it flows along the ground following the contour of the land. Upon reaching a low area, such as a trench, it descends into the trench filling it with gas.

The gas was first used on the Eastern Front during the winter of 1915. It proved to be of limited success because the sub-zero temperatures impacted the dissipation of the gas. This problem didn't exist with the warm April temperatures of the Western Front, making the results strikingly different.

Since the Hague Treaty of 1899 prohibited the use of projectiles containing poisonous gas, the Germans calculated that they were not in violation if they delivered the gas via cylinders. On April 22, 1915, the enemy soldiers strategically staged, then opened, the valves on fifty-seven hundred canisters of gas. The canisters were positioned so that the wind would carry the gas towards the Allied lines.

The enemy initiated the attack by launching a massive bombardment of the Allied trenches. During the shelling, the gas was released with the wind carrying it towards its intended target. Since it was common for an attack to be preceded by heavy shelling, the Allied forces were in their trenches waiting to repel the anticipated attack. The bombardment produced dark, heavy clouds of smoke that prevented the Allies from spotting the approaching gas until it was too late.

The Allied troops were expecting to see waves of enemy soldiers crossing the battlefield. Instead they saw a low, greenish-yellow mist rolling towards them. The gas cloud permeated four miles of trenches, affecting some ten thousand soldiers. It took only about ten minutes for half of the exposed troops to die.

The German Army hadn't gauged the potential effectiveness of the gas. As a result, they neglected to have sufficient reserve troops in place. Without the additional troop strength, they were unable to take full advantage of the wide opening in the Allied line. Although the German troops captured a significant amount of ground, without sufficient re-serves to hold it, much of it was lost when the Allied army launched a counterattack.

Attempting to capitalize on the successful, introductory release of the gas, the Germans repeated the process two days later. On April 24, chlorine gas was used against the unsuspecting Canadian troops. Fortunately, the quick-thinking Canadians used urine-soaked handker-chiefs to cover their mouths and noses, lessening the impact of the gas.

The Germans visualized the annihilation of extensive numbers of Allied troops, instead they encountered a defiant Canadian force stand-ing its ground. Fierce fighting ensued, causing heavy losses on both sides.

By the end of May the relentless German Army had gained additional high ground. This forced the Allies' to consolidate their positions closer to the city of Ypres. After many attempts to capture the city failed, the enemy retaliated by shelling it. By the end of the war the entire city of Ypres was reduced to piles of rubble.

The Second Battle of Ypres cost the lives of sixty-nine thousand Allied soldiers and thirty-five thousand German troops. The significant contrast in the number of Allied deaths can be directly attributed to the Germans' use of chlorine gas.

Second battle of Ypres

Journal Entry - April 5th–23rd

We remained at our position and continued firing on the enemy's trenches and guns. Enemy aircraft were very active and often we had to stop firing so that we wouldn't be spotted.

Our observation station located in the brewery was a veritable death trap. It was continually shelled, but in spite of this, we stuck it out for four days. That is until one shell hit directly on the little cellar. The shell wounded Grogan and Smith (the two telephonists on duty), while Lieutenant Richie marvelously escaped injury. Later poor Grogan died, causing Smith to be so shook up that he was sent away.

We are now using the remains of a house, which we called the "Green House", for the observation post. It also was shelled repeatedly, but we had no further casualties. As far as action, nothing out of the ordinary happened, just the usual give and take between armies.

The batteries at our rear were shelled occasionally but nothing within harming distance of our guns. I can hear sounds of continual heavy fighting far away to our left towards Ypres and to our right towards La Bassee. By the sounds of it, there must be hard scrapping in progress on the French front.

April 24th

The battery received orders to move with all speed to Ypres. We marched immediately towards Ypres and billeted for the night near La Gorgue.

April 25th

Today we had a long march to Odderdum. I was ordered to go forwards with the billeting party.

There was very heavy fighting going on at Ypres. I heard that there was a gigantic German assault that caused the French to retreat, and at the same time, forced the Canadians to retire. The battle continued to rage fiercely all night. The sounds of heavy artillery fire were overwhelming.

April 26th

The battery started to march about 8:30 a.m., halting outside the town of Vlamertinghe. As the battery remained outside of the town, George, Collins, and I went with the CO to reconnoiter a position for the battery.

As we neared Ypres we could hear the hellish bombardment going on. While galloping along the road we witnessed dead horses, overturned Lorries,[15] and discarded equipment along both sides of the road. Hundreds of wounded were being carried down, or seen hobbling along, the road the best way they could.

As we directed our horses through the town, some disturbing sights met our eyes. It seemed that along every few yards of the road there was something dead, or bits and pieces of men and horses that had been blown apart during the bombardment.

Shells were still absolutely falling everywhere. The town was an inferno. It seemed that every second man we met was wounded. We said to each other, "I reckon we're on the last lap of this journey."

We found a likely position where a few old branches and some dugouts were still intact, about a half mile to the rear of St. Jean. Shells were bursting right over us, so we continued to search for a more favorable position. Yet everywhere we looked

---

15   **Lorry:** The British term for a small truck.

seemed to be the same. The captain wasn't comfortable with the area for there was practically no cover remaining.

We went a little closer to the town where a Canadian Officer stopped us and asked what we were wanting. When we explained that we were looking for a spot to bring the battery into position, he said, "For God's sakes, don't bring them here; this corner is hell itself. Get out of it as quick as you can." Shells were dropping all around us. It seemed astounding that none of us had gotten hit.

Afterwards I learned that this part of the town was called "Dead Man's Corner". It deserved the name, for many dead were there about.

We left the Canadian and returned to our prior position. We decided it would have to suffice for all places seemed to be equally vulnerable.

While the remainder of the battery was approaching, we started to lay out a wire to a likely observation spot. George took a couple of chaps to start from the observation station while Collins, Billison, and I ran wire from the battery position through the village of St. Jean. We managed to reach the village unharmed, but like everywhere else, it was being heavily shelled.

I was jumping over a small stream that was by the church when a large shell burst almost on us. We took shelter behind a building. We could not move an inch due to all the shrapnel bullets flying about. It was miserable, for we had to remain there for an hour as shells continued to fall.

I noticed that just a few yards from us an artillery man and his horse were lying dead. Nearby was a smashed motor ambulance with the driver burned to a cinder. The ambulance's petrol tank must have ignited when it was hit by a shell. A na-

tive from one of our battalions lay dead in a ditch. At the end of the building there were several other corpses.

After a time the shelling abated a little, allowing us to start moving again. I met up with George, who had been in much the same terrible show as we had gone through. I was thirsty and thankfully managed to get a drink of water.

As we made our way back, we didn't get far before the shelling started again. We ran for our previous little shelter and gained it just in time. Shells were bursting very near and I asked Collins, "What is that strong, stinking smell?" My eyes were watering and we all three began coughing. We decided to chance it and go anywhere away from where we were.

After an exciting half-hour we got to the guns, but by that time I felt very sick. Afterwards we learned from an officer that it was due to the gas shells the Germans were using.

Author's note: I questioned the entry, "Afterwards we learned from an officer that it was due to gas shells the Germans were using". Since I'm not an expert about this topic, I decided to post the question on the World War One website, *Great War Forum*. My inquiry: "Would my grandfather have been exposed to chlorine or mustard gas?" The replies I received pointed out that mustard gas wasn't used until later in the war, in 1917. It would have been doubtful that he would have received a dose of chlorine gas because of his location during this period.

I remained curious as to the type of gas exposure he experienced, as well as to the method of delivery. Upon further researching the topic, it came to light that the Germans had used fragmentation shells filled with irritants against the British in the Battle of Neuve Chapelle. The irritant used was similar to that of tear gas, which would explain my grandfather's symptoms of watering eyes, vomiting and so on.

April 26th, continued

It was very lucky that we hurried to get out of it when we did or undoubtedly the three of us would have been gassed properly instead of partially. As it was I had enough gas to sufficiently stop me from eating anything for three days.

Shelling around the guns was getting pretty warm but we started to return fire in good style. The wire broke three times, and each time communications was lost with the forward observer. Normally in this case the batteries would stop firing. However, it was agreed that if we lost communications, we would raise the range of our guns.

During the afternoon I traveled through St. Jean and while doing so I became uneasy, dreading any further exposure to the gas. The reoccurring images of my previous gas experience made me anxious and tense. By the time I returned at nightfall, I thought I had been very fortunate to make it through the day.

The enemy kept up hard shelling everywhere. It sounded like one continual roar of shells bursting over us, with bullets and splinters knocking lumps off of my dugout. I really thought that this place might be the finishing touch. Of all the places I had been throughout the campaign, this was by far the worst. It seemed impossible for one to live long in it.

I had a few hours' sleep, yet was awakened now and again when a large shell burst somewhere nearby. At daylight we were at it again. The first thing that met George this morning was a shell dropping just the other side of the hedge. It fell among what had been a Canadian Battery Wagon line.

It didn't matter that the shell fell there, because most of the men had been killed when the Germans bayoneted them while they slept. The enemy also hung a Canadian officer to a barn and used bayonets to crucify a sergeant of the Canadian Scottish army to the barn door.

The Canadians' wagon line once had 200 horses and now only a dozen horses remain. If this wasn't enough, all of the

Canadian guns were captured by the enemy. All this happened when the Germans broke through our lines the previous week.

Later the Canadians were revenged through a magnificent charge by their infantry. They are considered to be fine fellows and splendid fighters. They hated the Germans and cursed them for their murderous ways of waging war.

I was told that a couple of days previous the Canadian Scottish were ordered to retire, but refused to do so. Instead of retiring as ordered, they charged the enemy on their own. It was a mad thing to do for they lost over 500 men, although they captured 100 or more prisoners.

I dare say that not one of the captured Germans was brought down as a prisoner. All the soldiers in the Allied Armies started fighting like the enemy, no quarter given, and the Canadians gave none. As evidence of this, just to the rear of our guns, there was the corpse of a husky Prussian guardsman - a fine figure of a man who stood fully at 6 foot 3 inches in height. The Canadians had pinned him to a tree with a bayonet. They stuck a postcard on his forehead that said, "Canada does not forget!" Then someone had written, "We'll give them crucify" next to the word "Canada".

The cruel and barbaric happenings around this period would fill a book with horrors of all descriptions. The merciless style of war created by the Germans carried over to their enemy. The centuries that it has taken to develop the meaning behind the word "civilized" has only taken a couple of years to reduce to "barbaric."

I was pleased with the splendid fighting of both the Canadians and the Indian troops and proud that they were fighting with us. By the end of November, truly enough Canadians had served in the battle of Ypres as did the 7th, 8th, and 1st British Divisions.

April 27th

The shelling and firing continued today at about the same level as yesterday. The only difference was that the enemy started to send over their great 17 inch Howitzer shell into Ypres. These mammoth shells were hitting our artillery and infantry over a mile to our rear. The Germans must have been preparing for this battle for months because the amount of ammunition they were launching at us was increasing.

George and I found another observation post near St. Julien. It was located in the remains of a house about 200 yards in the rear of our trenches. However, it was almost useless for our wire was constantly getting broken. Its location made it impossible to use signal flags.

Our captain was a perfect brick. He stuck it out with us until he got carried away when one shrapnel burst landed nearby. The burst caused him to leave the house and run to the safety of a fire trench. Right after his departure a 17 inch came right into the house and almost propelled it into the air.

When the smoke cleared, the house was reduced to a pile of wreckage. Several natives had been killed, but Captain Donahue was fine having made a lucky escape. Three natives were horribly wounded and were pinned down under the wreckage. An officer mercifully shot them to put them out of their misery.

With our observation post destroyed, we continued to fire the rest of the day using a map. During the day several shells fell on us. One pitched right in the heart of George's wagon. Luckily nobody was hurt.

In the afternoon the thought struck me that it was my birthday.... Gee! It was a very grim and bloody one! Old George and Collins had an exciting afternoon while going along the wire. They were forced to take refuge in a shell hole and had to stay in it for a long while. They eventually got back safely.

About midnight on the 27th, we got orders to move at once to a position that was absolutely suicidal to hold. The battery got away all right but I remained behind, along with my horse holder, Albert. We were waiting for George and Collins to return from infantry headquarters where they went to reel in what remained of our wire.

While waiting for George and Collins to return, I was entertained by the combination of bursting shells, artillery fire, and rockets being launched from both our and the Germans' trenches. They lit up the heavens like a gigantic fireworks display, similar to the ones I watched as a child. I waited behind the shelter of a building for what seemed a long time. After a while I started to think that they must have gotten knocked over, so I resolved to go and look for them.

It was a nasty job as the road to the village of St. Jean was being heavily shelled. Even though the road was deserted I crept from tree to tree for protection from shrapnel. Everywhere I stepped there were dead horses and an occasional body.

When I got to the village, two infantry chaps were coming down from the other end of the village. I asked them if they had seen anything of my chums, and they denied seeing anyone. They advised me to go no further if I wanted to live. Taking their advice I decided to return to where I had left the horses, thinking that George and Collins were goners.

I was greatly relieved to find that they had returned safely. They told me that they had chosen to come back a different way, because it was too hot to go through the village and walk on the road. I thought to myself, "Good show, old chaps" We returned to our battery.

I had hardly been back 10 minutes when a shell struck the roof of the shed. Unfortunately we were inside when the tiles, bricks, etc. fell in on us like a shower. George and I escaped injury, but Collins got a whack in the shoulder although it was not serious. Nineteen shells followed, all within 40 yards of us. It was amazing that not one of us was touched.

The shells seemed to decrease their range on the road leading through Ypres. Therefore we resolved to go for it and did so with the maddest gallop I had ever requested from my steed!

My old charger never moved so quickly as when we galloped round "Dead Man's Gulch". On our way through town we didn't encounter anyone, just dead horses and bodies. We made it through without mishap. But our troubles for this night were not over yet.

I had only a faint idea of where our battery was going. We continued to follow the road until meeting a point where it split. Unaware of the battery's direction, I opted to proceed to the right. Eventually we found ourselves just on the left of hill 60, which was being subjected to a fierce bombardment from all directions. At this point I knew I had selected the wrong road. We turned around and made a mad ride back to where the two roads joined, taking the alternate route.

We didn't ride very far when we found a reel of wire alongside the road. It must have fallen off one of the wagons, so I knew we were on the right track. Eventually we caught up with the battery just as dawn was breaking.

April 28th

We went into action on the edge of some woods located on the left of Ypres. This spot seemed quieter than the place we had just vacated.

In the afternoon George and I ran our wire to an observation point just over the canal. Everywhere I looked was a scene of desolation. There were half-starved cattle and pigs roaming about or lying dead. Along with the animals all sorts of farm commodities were tossed about.

The French infantry had held this front and just to the rear of the trenches were four of their abandoned Howitzers, indicating how far the enemy had advanced.

We stopped to observe some big shells that were bursting near us. This was the first time we had experienced this type of shell. We promptly named it "Black Jack" because of the great volume of black smoke it gave off. While we were watching, one these shells burst directly over the heads of a few Frenchmen. It scattering them even though I didn't think any of them were harmed.

When we got back to the battery the large caliber shells were continually passing right over our guns. Only one fell near me, landing about 20 yards from where I had made my dugout.

During the night two batteries of French 7.5 inch guns took a position about 50 yards in our rear.

April 29th

Our wire was broken in several places from the continuous shelling. It had been impossible to get to the observation post. We had to use maps and wireless communication between us and the observation airplanes in order to fire.

We must have been spotted by an enemy observation airplane, for the German artillery gave it to us warm in the afternoon.

In the evening the officers made a bivouac beneath a layer of trees, just a few yards on my left. A few shells, real coal-boxes, were bursting very near the officers, so they moved into a dugout further over to the left. This was good fortune because a few minutes later a shell hit the tree and snapped it like a match.

Since other shells followed we had to leave the guns for a while. When the shelling was over, we went back to where the officer's dugout had been. The hits had blown the place to pieces. The two coats that hung on the tree were absolutely in ribbons and almost everything else was ruined.

One of the officers had been sitting on a box of biscuits that was now blown yards away. The box was reduced to a piece of twisted metal with not even one biscuit remaining. Everything was almost unrecognizable, including the bodies of the officers.

Mr. Dowling, one of the officer's servants, got both his arms badly splintered. All night the enemy continually shelled the roads to our right rear.

April 30th

This morning we still didn't have communication with the observation post, so we used wireless communication with one of the observation airplanes. Our goal was to fire a bombardment in support of an attack by the French, which was said to be successful.

In the afternoon we were expecting a German counterattack after being heavily shelled.

The 57th who were just a little ways on our right got it worse than us. One shell pitched into their communications dugout, killing four telephonists and leaving several men wounded. They got it so fiercely that they were compelled to desert their guns, as we did yesterday. In spite of this they soon returned.

The French napped[16] (as per usual) when one 17 inch shell dropped by their guns. Several shells fell in front of us. One shell dropped 30 yards from our left gun where I was standing. It is impossible to describe these monsters coming through the air. They sound like an express train going through a tunnel. When they burst, it is like a terrific clap of thunder causing the earth to sway, as if shaken by a small earthquake.

Later we measured one of the shell holes. Amazingly, it was 25 feet deep and 43 feet across. The force of the explosion scattered lumps of earth and rock many yards from the shell hole. It seems impossible, even to someone like me who understands artillery, that this great eruption could have been made by a shell. We picked up several shell splinters that weighed anywhere from a few ounces to several pounds.

The Germans' counterattack was repulsed and towards dark it became a little quieter, except for the usual nightly, dozen per hour shellings.

The Germans' 17 inch shells must have put the wind up the Frenchies, for they moved during the night and never came back.

May 1st–4th

We continued to fire from the same position even though the enemy was shelling us constantly day and night.

During attacks and counterattacks, which go on twice daily, we directed our fire mostly by using the wireless to communicate with an observation airplane.

On May 3rd the gun batteries on our left seemed to get it jolly hot. In spite of the gases and their preponderance of artillery, we were informed that we had stopped their march on Calais.

---

16   Napped was a slang term meaning they fled.

We were ordered to move with the Lahore Division (which was now sadly depleted in numbers) on the night of the 4th.

Mr. Donahue and I left about 5:00 p.m. and after a hard ride found billets some 1.5 miles from Ypres, in a village whose name I never learned. I left at midnight to conduct the battery to the new billet.

All night I rode through the rain on my way back to the battery. As I passed through a small village, I decided to stop and try to find something to eat and drink. I tied my horse to the railings of a churchyard, then walked around determined to find something. After a while I came upon an establishment and vigorously knocked on the door. The door opened slowly. On the other side of the door was a staff officer. I think he was as surprised as I was.

He asked me what I wanted and I replied that I was searching for something to eat and drink. He was very good-natured about my intrusion and motioned me inside. To my pleasant surprise he then fixed me up with a much appreciated meal. Upon finishing I left. Even though it was still raining and cold I felt refreshed.

About 4:30 a.m. I met up with the battery and guided them to the village. We arrived at the billet about 6:00 a.m. where I got some breakfast from the officer's cook of the Ammunition Column. After a long night and a good breakfast, I was exhausted so I found a place to lay down and slept until about 10:00 a.m.

May 5th

After a couple of hours of rest I proceeded to secure a new billet with Mr. Woods, in the direction of the town of Estaires. This proved to be a long ride. We located a good spot. I had a little dispute with the farmer, which delayed me from fixing up billets before 7:00 p.m. However, after a stern threat and the help of an interpreter, I managed to secure the place for the battery. Mr. Woods volunteered to ride back to conduct the battery to the billet.

Fatigue had set in. After caring for my charger, I went in a barn and dropped just as I was into a sound sleep.

The battery arrived at dawn. After organizing them I was informed that our orders were changed. The battery was to take up our old position at Croix Barbette by nightfall in support of an attack in the region of Festubert. The orders to march were received in better spirits by the farmer than I.

May 6th

It was a beautiful day which I spent mostly in a much needed sleep. After I woke up I moved the battery over to our old position, arriving about 7:30 p.m. We were replacing a section of the 30th Battery. Then it dawned on me, it was here that I had left my mattress. I was elated to find that my woolen mattress was still where I left it.

CHAPTER EIGHT:

OPPORTUNITIES NOT TAKEN

May 6, 1915, was my grandfather's last journal entry, for reasons that remain unknown. He was transferred from France on September 1, 1915.

Further research brought to light a military document dated May, 1916. It made reference to the fact that Second Lieutenant F. Coxen was temporarily transferred to the Mersey defense district in England. His orders were to carry out the inspection of the antiaircraft gun detachments.

On June 9, 1916, he was appointed adjutant and quartermaster of the 47th AA Company, Royal Garrison Artillery (RGA), and awarded the temporary rank of captain. He maintained this position until November, 1916, at which time it appears he returned to his RFA group.

On 28 November 1917 he was transferred back to France. He was assigned to AA battery and remained in France until May 18, 1918.

He was appointed to the 253rd Squadron, Royal Air Force (RAF), at Bembridge on January 12, 1918. While carrying out his duties as observer officer, his responsibilities were elevated to being placed in charge of the RAF pay department. He remained with the 253rd Squadron until its disbandment in May 1, 1919.

While stationed in England, my grandfather had sufficient opportunities to contact the families of his three deceased comrades. However, he neglected to act upon these occasions, which led me to a haunting question; "Why didn't he keep his promise?" This query repeatedly emerged whenever my frustration level reached its peak.

Eventually, the importance of establishing why he didn't fulfill his promise became as critical to me as trying to complete it. A fuller understanding of the forces shaping those choices gradually evolved while proofing the transcribed journal.

Without the interference of trying to decipher my grandfather's handwriting, I was able to absorb the feelings behind his words. Reading his journal allowed for greater insight into his personality, ethics and character. By traveling along on my grandfather's war journey throughout Belgium and France, I was able to identify those events that had a larger impact upon him than others.

Obtaining this insight exposed the obvious dilemma he faced in keeping the promise: whether to relay the disturbing, traumatic accounts of death, or to submerge these gruesome realities in order to live. I could highly assume that the totality of these dreadful experiences, including witnessing the tragic deaths of two of his friends, created images he didn't want to revisit. Suppressing these visions most likely fed his frequent nightmares.

Much has been written and discussed regarding surviving soldiers exposed to the horrors of war, who prefer to lock away these memories of destruction and carnage. I found this to be the case with my uncles after World War II. It continues to be true for soldiers returning from deployment in Iraq and Afghanistan.

Enlightened by these revelations, I've concluded that my grandfather was unable to confront the families of George, Pudgie and Bobby. This insight enabled me to refocus on finding potential living relatives.

CHAPTER NINE:

SEARCHING FOR GEORGE BRAMWELL

The last research paper I wrote was 1965, when I was a senior in high school. For the benefit of those that didn't grow-up during the 60s, researching a subject was an exhausting process. A great deal of time was spent in libraries, thumbing through the Dewey decimal system and card catalog to locate numerous research books. The Internet didn't exist - hell, personal computers didn't exist!

At the onset of my research in 2008, I had at my disposal both a laptop and the Internet to access a wealth of information. The problem I faced was where to begin. It is one thing to research a subject, but how do you find information about a person that died one-hundred years ago?

I decided to focus on World War One websites. I felt that they would offer me the background and knowledge about the war that would be the most helpful. It didn't take me long to discover that the UK had the most numerous and best websites dealing with World War One. Since my grandfather served in the British army, I felt that the UK sites would be the most beneficial source.

The first site I explored was called, "The Long, Long Trail." The information contained on this website offered me the knowledge and foundation necessary to search further. The site even offered links to other helpful websites.

One suggested site was the British National Archives, which is helpful in locating military information on a particular soldier. Since this was my purpose, I clicked on the website link and became instantly trapped within a digital maze. My analogy in describing this phenomenon is that of being stuck in a rowboat, with one oar, in the middle of an ocean. It doesn't matter how hard you row, you always end up where you started.

The National Archives definitely contains a kingdom of information. However, to find that of which you seek, requires the knowledge of what key is needed to open the appropriate door.

During my research I've become a member of countless WWI websites and logged many hours posting pleas for help. In the beginning I searched collectively for information on all three chums, a strategy proving to be both stressful and non-productive. Therefore I refined my search to that of George Bramwell. Thinking, perhaps by uncovering data on George, I could utilize the same process to find the other two.

I spent a great deal of time rummaging through the National Archives without success. I should restate this; I found listings for several George Bramwells but their information didn't match the George I was seeking. By referring to the journal I knew the date of George's death. I keyed in this date, along with George's first and last name, into the World War One Commonwealth War Graves Commission's website. The results produced a few George Bramwells, but their records did not correspond with the facts contained within the journal.

Exploring other avenues I found a World War One book website. I perused through their book selections in hopes of finding one about the Royal Field Artillery. Instead, I discovered they offered a DVD that listed all British soldiers who died during World War One. Their pitch was enticing in that the disk was searchable. BINGO! The disk was expensive, even in pounds, let alone in US currency. I was desperate at this point. Determining that if it contained a complete list of soldiers it might be worth the expense.

Following the lengthy shipping period, I ripped open the box and stuffed the DVD into my laptop. My anticipation for success grew as the program downloaded. When the program opened with an error message, my frustration was beyond description noting that it required an earlier version of Windows. My mind flew through scenarios for a solution. It dawned on me that I owned another machine with the necessary software. Hallelujah - a successful download!

I was flabbergasted to find that the program contained the same limited search fields as the Commonwealth's website. In ordering the DVD, I had envisioned using the program's brigade field to locate deceased soldiers from the 43rd Brigade.

My limited options forced me to expand the search to all soldiers who perished around a given date, with the last name of Bramwell. This produced several outcomes. To narrow down the choices, I reviewed the burial information on each one. The process was tedious, but I found a soldier named Percy Bramwell who served in the fortieth battery of the RFA. The date listed was within a day of George's demise. I thought to myself, "What would be the odds of two soldiers with the last name Bramwell dying within the same day and battery?" I was confident that Percy was the man I was looking for.

Included in Percy's burial records were the names and addresses of both his wife and parents. With this new information in hand, I visited Ancestor.com to track down the appropriate family tree. Those that develop family trees create an e-mail account and input personal family data. They can also choose whether to keep the family tree private or make it public. I was delighted to find a public Bramwell family tree, allowing me to search for Percy.

I was on a roll. Not only did I find the Bramwell family tree, but I also found Percy's name listed under his parents. Unfortunately, the owner hadn't included anything beyond listing Percy and his parents. I was pleased to be able to include an account of Percy's death under his name. Although satisfying, I still hadn't met the terms of the promise by making contact with a relative.

I sent an email to the owner of the Bramwell family tree, explaining the details of the promise and Percy's death. Within this correspondence I included my e-mail address and requested a response. After three weeks without a reply I decided to pursue this avenue further. Accessing Ancestry.com I found the owner's name and place of residence. Upon further investigation I was able to obtain his address and phone number. I briefly considered calling him. Social discretion prevailed, so I opted instead to send him a letter.

Weeks went by without a word. I was about to close the case on George/Percy Bramwell, when I surprisingly received the anticipated e-mail. It wasn't what I'd hoped for, but it was a response. The Bramwell genealogist apologized for taking so long to contact me. He explained that he was developing several family trees, but had determined not to continue research on the Bramwell line. As verified by his extensive research, there appeared to be no living relatives from Percy's lineage. I now considered the Bramwell promise to be fulfilled.

A copy of the e-mail is as follows:

Dear Mr. Coxen:

Pardon my delay in responding. You're correct when you point out that I don't check my Bramwell tree often. It's only one of about a dozen trees that I try to maintain on ancestry.com. I probably won't be able to spend the time to really keep them all up to date until I retire in 2013.

Most of the work that I've done on the Bramwells was done during the summer of 2009. My purpose was to extend the family line back into the 1700's in Stockport, where I believe the name could have been Bramwell-Bramhall-Bramall, etc. I've brought some of the Bramwell lines down to the 1901 Census for completeness (using mainly census records).

My review of the info I have on Percy Bramwell was that he was my second cousin, 4 times removed; actually quite distant. Our most recent common ancestor was Benjamin Bramwell (c 1779 -1848). All of my contacts have been with descendants of Benjaimn Bramwell's son, George Bramwell (b 1806). He was an older brother of Peter Bramwell (b 1821), Percy's grandfather. I don't have any information on any relatives of Peter, nor of Peter's son (and Percy's father), Sydney Bramwell (b 1857). I don't know if there are any descendants alive today of the Peter Bramwell branch of the family.

My ancestor, Benjamin T. Bramwell, came to the US about 160 years ago, so we've obviously lost contact with the English side of the family long ago.

I don't know if you'll be able to find any close relatives of Percy Bramwell...

CHAPTER TEN:

IN SEARCH OF PUDGIE AND BOBBY

Finding George/Percy Bramwell had been burdensome, but it was even more difficult to find any information on the other two chums. After spending a considerable amount of time on the task, I came up with the brilliant idea of taking my story to the airwaves.

I enjoy listening to National Public Radio (NPR). One of my favorite programs is *The Story*. The program is about an hour in length and consists of two different human interest stories. The show provides people with an opportunity to tell their tales.

While listening to a segment on my way home from work, it dawned on me that I had my own great story to tell. Perhaps if aired, some aspect of it might trigger a listener's memory.

That evening I went to NPR's website. I found the web page describing the process of submitting a story, then keyed in the necessary information. Unsure of whether I'd be contacted, I busied myself with other pursuits.

About a week later I received a phone call from the program director. After complementing my entry, she proceeded to ask me a few questions about its content. Towards the end of the conversation, she requested that I bring both the journal and the letter to their station the next day. Since the station is located an hour away in Chapel Hill, North Carolina, I agreed. I naturally assumed that they wanted to examine the journal and letter to validate my story's authenticity. What transpired, however, was very different.

The next morning I arrived at the station with documentation in hand. After a brief meeting with the director, she informed me that I would soon meet with Dick Gordon to tape the interview. This startling announcement falls within the top ten surprises in my life. (The top spot is awarded to my wife, who at the age of forty, revealed that she was pregnant.)

Panic could have been an issue, although there wasn't enough time to allow it to get a firm grip. I was ushered into the recording studio to meet with Dick, a pleasant, engaging man, with a disposition that relaxes his guests. He explained the taping process and instructed me as to how to talk clearly into the microphone.

Intently preoccupied with providing intelligent responses, the remainder of the session is hazy. The staff assured me that any rough spots would be edited, exuding confidence that I would be pleased with the results.

About a week later the program director informed me that my spot would air on February 9th. Expounding further, she asserted that the staff had been moved by the power of the story, especially the journal entries. She enthusiastically added that an actor with a British accent had been hired to recite selected excerpts, stressing that this addition made the story even more compelling.

Afterwards my wife and I urged everyone we knew to listen to *The Story* on the appointed date. Like a kid at Christmas, I could hardly wait to listen to the program. On February 9th my wife and I were glued to the radio. Following the broadcast we both agreed that the actor selected for the journal readings did, indeed, bring the diary to life.

Once the program aired, it was a few weeks before the station emailed me a couple of audience leads. I soon concluded that they were not worth pursuing. Although the broadcast didn't result in further leads, I was pleased to have used this format.

It was left up to me to find Pudgie Taylor and Bobby Glue. Without Pudgie's real first name, finding the correct Taylor amongst the hundreds that served in the British Army, would be like finding a Taylor in a haystack. On the other hand, a soldier with the last name of "Glue" had promise. I optimistically proceeded to employ all the previously mentioned strategies to uncover facts regarding Bobbie's war years.

Using the DVD of British war casualties, I performed a search for "Bobby Glue" that produced zero results. Then I experienced an epiphany – Bobby is a nickname for Robert. Repeating the query using "Robert Glue" gave me the same results. In hopes of obtaining the same positive outcome achieved using the last name "Bramwell", I keyed in "Glue", The quest was still unproductive.

At this point I decided to return to World War One websites having faith that someone in cyberspace would contribute to my mission. This too proved to be ineffective. Coming up empty-handed on Bobby, I returned to the same websites looking for Pudgie.

First on the agenda was the British site, *RootsChat*. The site allows members to post and respond to questions about World War One. I posted a request for help finding Pudgie.

A day or two passed before I received a couple of replies. One knowledgeable respondent posted a list of Taylors who died in World War One. He also suggested I visit an informative website, *Great War Forum*. I perused his list of Taylors for any tidbit of information providing a link back to Pudgie. Frustrated with the lack of progress, I decided to momentarily retire from the project.

A few days later I was reviewing my extensive list of World War One websites. I questioned the wisdom of expanding this collection by one more. There is a fine line between wisdom and stupidity. Dwelling on the complexity of bridging the philosophical differences, caused me to lean more towards the wisdom of adding the site. This decision was soon validated. In assessing my existing websites as "limbs yielding little fruit", why not branch out in a new direction?

Performing a search for the *Great War Forum* placed me at the site's main page; it appeared to be well laid-out. To evaluate the quality of the site, I reviewed a few pages, paying close attention to the detail of the responses to posted questions. This element is of considerable importance because many forum sites contain ideal chatter.

Following the standard routine for becoming a member, I was surprised after clicking the submit button to receive a pop-up message stating, "Your request for membership will be reviewed; you'll be informed via e-mail if you've been accepted." This type of format seemed unusual. I facetiously wondered if a background check was required for membership.

Once conditions were met, I posted my inquiry, requesting data on both Bobbie and Pudgie. From past experience, it usually takes a while for a reply - if any are forthcoming. To my elated surprise, a response eventually popped up. Even better, this was no ordinary response; it contained quite a bit of information.

While digesting the content of the first reply, I immediately received two more. The original response listed five soldiers with the last name of Taylor, all serving in the RFA in 1914: two drivers, a trumpeter, a bombardier, and a veteran of the Boer War. Despite this hopeful news, the respondent neglected to obtain any information about Bobby Glue. I sat in awe, staring at my screen, wondering why I'd waited so long to join this forum.

Seizing this fresh opportunity, I examined the military records of the five Taylor candidates. Not one of them had served in the 43rd Brigade with my grandfather, so I originally defined this as another disappointingly false lead.

Upon further thought, I speculated that the four chums may have been in different batteries or brigades. This hypothesis would explain why Pudgie's name never appeared within the timely entries of my grandfather's journal, and why Bobby Glue's name only emerged at the time of his death. Fred and Bobby found themselves occupying the same battlefield location, at a point when grandfather temporarily transferred over to the 51st battery to receive training on an 18 lb. gun.

Following this scenario, one recorded Taylor could be Pudgie. But which one? Expanding upon this line of reasoning, my focus returned to grandfather's letter detailing the promise. He noted that Pudgie was killed during the Battle of Ypres. Assuming that it was the First Battle of Ypres, I posted the question, "How many Taylors were killed during the First Battle of Ypres?" The responder, a member of the *Great War Forum* group, "Old Sweats", stated that, "There were forty-five Taylors killed during the First Battle of Ypres, and eight were Royal Navy (RN). Of the thirty-seven remaining Taylors, only one man served in the Royal Horse Artillery/Royal Artillery (RHA/RA), and he had served in the Fourteenth Brigade, not the 43rd."

This knowledge assisted in narrowing down possible contenders. Yet without additional specifics, it became impossible to confirm which Taylor had been a participant in the promise. Too many questions lingered for which I had no means to resolve. Even with the assistance of my most reliable source, the "Old Sweats" on the *Great War Forum,* definitive statistics on Pudgie Taylor continued to elude me.

With the journal illuminating the date and battlefield location of Bobby Glue's demise, it was logical to attach his duty assignment to the 51st battery. Even though armed with this reasonable deduction, there were no soldiers within this particular military grouping bearing his name. In fact, as far as I can determine, there is no listing of a "Bobby Glue", perishing in Ypres, Belgium, on any British World War One military records.

I had received immense help in my endeavor to track down this unknown soldier. Although the participants were very willing to take on an attainable challenge, each source involved could not truly determine if "Bobby Glue" was the authentic name of a soldier or a nickname. Once again, I had reached a dead end.

For three years, I have dedicated myself to finding living relatives of George Bramwell, Pudgie Taylor, and Bobby Glue. I'm confident that I unearthed records for George/Percy Bramwell and made contact with a distant relative. Therefore, I've completed at least one promise.

Even though the hunt for Pudgie Taylor has been narrowed, I am still unable to authenticate that any recorded data belongs to the fallen soldier mentioned in my grandfather's promise letter. The documented existence of a warrior named Bobbie Glue escapes my pursuit. I've reconciled to the fact that the promise made to Bobby and Pudgie may sadly remain unfulfilled.

Contrasting the accomplishments met to the original goals set, I realize that I have underperformed my expectations. Nevertheless, I find solace in having made a successful connection with one family. In my heart I feel that my grandfather would be proud of my perseverance and perhaps even comment, "Jolly good show, Grandson!"

CHAPTER ELEVEN:

THE IMPORTANCE OF STORIES

I've learned a great deal while writing this book, but the most significant lesson is the importance of people writing down their personal stories. I used to believe that I didn't have stores to tell, or at least not important ones. I have since discovered that this belief is false. I now realize that our stories are created from the daily experiences of life. We consider some to be eventful, while most are not. Combined together over time, our stories take on patterns that define who we are and what we believe.

Many Native American tribes know the importance of maintaining tales or legends. It is a way to pass down their tribal history and keep their ancestors alive. Yarns are told around campfires with the young sitting wide-eyed, listening to tales of brave battles, animal hunts, and tribal events. Some tales were etched onto animal hides, in order to be visibly passed down to future generations. These tribes realized that unrecorded stories die with their creators.

Through my research and exposure to my grandfather's journal, I've been inspired by the rewarding aspect of recorded stories, as well as the regret that can stem from unrecorded ones. The pleasure of reading my grandfather's journal epitomizes the joy that can be derived from possessing such a family treasure.

I didn't know my grandfather very well. He presented himself as stern and unapproachable, the type of person who might be likely to carry a sign with "Children Keep Away" written on it. In addition to his formidable demeanor, he and my grandmother spent a greater portion of their retirement years at their home in Florida, only visiting during the summer months to escape the Florida heat. I can only remember a few times that I actually interacted with him during my formative years.

My grandfather's journal is a prime example of the value of documenting events in one's life. It has been through his writings that I've gotten to know the man behind the stoic exterior, presenting me with a peek into his tender, loving side. Reading his war experiences has helped me define his true character. For this, I'm eternally grateful.

After my father passed away in 2006, I experienced a feeling of loss, not only for my parent but also for his personal history. Shortly after his death, my brother, sister, and I had to dispense of the items within our childhood home. In the process we went through some of my father's personal belongings. We were surprised by what he'd kept: high school diplomas, his military draft card, some personal letters, and many other items.

As we determined what to keep and what to discard, it occurred to me that each of these stored items was meaningful to my father. They must have represented a significant memory or special story. Holding his draft card, I was transcended to the day when I received my own.

I was a single young man, just out of high school when the Vietnam War was heating up. I could vividly recall the intense anxiety that touched the lives of all males 18 years and older - facing the reinstatement of military conscription. Assigned a draft number based on one's birth date, the relatively high number of "224" will always hold a special place in my heart. That particular numeral spared me from being randomly called up for active duty.

My father's World War Two draft card symbolized an entirely different story for him, that of a new father pulled into an alarming, large-scale global conflict. Ironically, territory marked by the footsteps and corpses of soldiers engaged in the First World War continued to be fought over by later combatants of my father's era. There were so many possible stories that could be attached to this piece of paper. Yet, without my father, these accounts are only conjecture; the actual particulars are lost forever.

Only a few of my father's narratives remain—the ones he shared with us as we were growing up. Some were from his childhood, while others described his experiences while serving in the U.S. Navy during

World War Two. Even as I treasure these shared stories, I know that they are mere glimpses into a much fuller life, one I'll never know.

I'm gratified to realize that, on many occasions, my father and I created memories together. Among these are hunting and fishing episodes, Boy Scout camping trips, and residential construction projects. My plans are to draft a chronicle of these common experiences, where my father will remain alive within its sentimental pages.

I'm carrying this lesson forward in my own life. Even though I've had many personal conversations with my own children, I know that in time, their recollection of these anecdotal tales may fade. It will be comforting for me to seal these memories posthumously within my own journal, serving as a window into the man they called father.

Composing this book, *The Great Promise*, has embellished the value of my grandfather's journal much beyond that which could be derived by myself or any of his descendants. Its examination will transcend any reader beyond a mere historical depiction of World War One, transporting them through the personal experiences of one man who endured, while millions of others perished.

EPILOGUE

Following active duty my grandfather returned to his civilian occupation as an electrician. At one point he was involved in rewiring the Parliament Building and Buckingham Palace in London. There is a reliable family rumor that during the rewiring of the Parliament, my grandfather took a lunch break and sat on the throne of England while eating his cheese sandwich.

By 1922 climatic conditions in England had degraded, continuing to adversely affect my grandfather's lungs, already damaged by exposure to chlorine gas. This postwar environment drove a difficult decision to emigrate from England, with either the United States or Australia as appealing destinations. Many years later, during a conversation with my paternal uncle, I was astonished to learn that the Frederick Coxen family's destiny was determined in 1922 by the toss of a coin!

It was at this point that the family had boarded a ship bound for the United States out of Southampton, England. Upon arriving in New York harbor, they were processed through Ellis Island. The family moved to Detroit, Michigan, to stay with one of my grandfather's relatives. He worked in various jobs in the area until 1930, when he started his own company, Excelda Manufacturing.

Excelda primarily produced automotive polishes; one of its main customers was Ford Motor Company. As was common with many enterprises prior to World War II, in order to meet the growing needs of a country at war, my grandfather converted the business over to a tool and die shop. For a time, the facility manufactured parts for a military bomber being assembled in Detroit's Willow Run Airport. Excelda continues to be owned and managed by family members, retaining Ford Motor Company as an important customer.

To the best of my knowledge, there were at least two occasions when my grandparents returned to England to visit relatives. I don't believe he took advantage of these opportunities to fulfill the promise made at the onset of his active military duty. Conversations about his involvement in the *Great War*, involving either my active or inactive participation, never took place. The box of mementos is my only link to this phase of my grandfather's history.

I was thirteen when my grandfather died of lung cancer in 1960. The doctors attributed this fatality to damaging gas exposure during the war, combined with cigarette smoking. My grandmother remained with us for a few more years, at which point she was laid to rest with my grandfather in a small cemetery in Pompano Beach, Florida.

GLOSSARY

Bully Beef: Canned corned beef that was the principal protein ration of the British army.

Coal-box: A type of artillery shell used by the German Army that produced a great deal of black smoke when it exploded. The black smoke looked like the dust produced when a box of coal is dropped.

Envelope: To be surrounded and captured by the enemy

Garhwali: A group of people who primarily live in the Garhwal Himalayas of the northern Indian state of Uttarakhand.

Gurkhas: A regiment of the British and Indian armies comprised of people from Nepal.

Jack Johnson: The nickname given to a German artillery shell. It was named after the boxer, Jack Johnson, because he was very powerful and really packed a punch.

Keep: A stronghold or innermost fortified part of a castle.

Lorry: The British term for a small truck.

Lyddite: British explosive used for filling artillery shells in World War One. Actually molten and cast picric acid.

Parapet: The side of the trench facing the enemy.

Redoubt: A temporary fortification built to defend a position.

Salient: The trench system projecting toward the enemy.

Semaphore Flag: Hand-held flags that are used to send visual messages.

Territorials: Spare time volunteer force of the British Army

Tommy: Slang word for a British soldier.

2645218R00082

Printed in Great Britain
by Amazon.co.uk, Ltd.,
Marston Gate.